CHURCHILL
his paintings

CHURCHILL
his paintings

A Catalog compiled by David Coombs

Foreword by Lady Spencer-Churchill

The World Publishing Company

Cleveland and New York

Published by The World Publishing Company
2231 West 110th Street, Cleveland, Ohio 44102

Library of Congress Catalog Number 67–24472

This book was designed and produced by George Rainbird Ltd,
Marble Arch House, 44 Edgware Road, London, W.2, England

House editor: Jocelyn Selson
Designer: George Sharp
Indexer: H. V. Molesworth Roberts

Color origination: Schwitters, Zurich, Switzerland
Westerham Press Ltd, Kent, England
Printed by Westerham Press Ltd, Kent
Bound by the Wigmore Bindery Ltd, London, England

CONTENTS

For more than forty years,

my husband pursued the art of painting,

with all his customary energy and zeal.

His pictures have now been brought together

and illustrated in this catalogue,

whose publication will, I hope,

enable many people to share something of

the immense pleasure and stimulation

that my husband so often found in art.

Clementine Spencer-Churchill

Note Color plates bear Roman numerals with Arabic numerals in brackets. The latter refer to the relevant catalog entry in the monochrome section.

It should be emphasized that it has so far not been possible to establish with any certainty an accurate date for a number of the pictures.

INTRODUCTION

Although only one man is proclaimed on the title page as the compiler, this book is in fact the result of a substantial co-operative labour.

Most of the catalogue is based on a list prepared, in the company of the compiler, by Mr R. H. Pawsey during the course of the probate valuation of Sir Winston Churchill's estate. Subsequently, considerable amendments were made by Lady Spencer-Churchill and Mrs Christopher Soames, who somehow found the time to examine, with Mr Pawsey, the many hundreds of pictures remaining at Chartwell so that their subjects could be identified and authenticity confirmed. The difficulty of dating most of the paintings, even approximately, was largely overcome with the help of Mr Frank Patrickson, framemaker to Sir Winston in his later years and conservor of many of his canvases.

Contrary to legend, Sir Winston gave away a great many of his paintings, not only to his family and friends, but also to his colleagues and members of his household. Some of these gifts were spontaneous, others solicited, but they amount in total to about a fifth of the whole. The discovery of the artist's prodigality would have spelt the end to any ambitions to reasonable completeness for this catalogue had it not been for the generous help of the Misses Hamblin, Pugh, Snelling and Chapman, all secretaries to Sir Winston, and the source of much invaluable information. A number of Sir Winston's paintings domiciled in the United States were brought together at the New York World's Fair in 1965, and Mrs Jane Welby, in the midst of many other cares, sent details of the pictures and arranged for them to be photographed.

The majority of the black and white photographs in this catalogue were taken by Mr Tony Fruish, of A. C. Cooper Ltd, who has helped the compiler in many ways, not least in travelling all over England photographing paintings and checking their particulars. His colleague, Mr Rodney Wright Watson, was responsible for most of the colour photographs.

To all these people, to my long-suffering colleagues on *The Connoisseur*, particularly Mr L. G. G. Ramsey, the Editor, to Miss Jocelyn Selson and the team that produced this book, to Mr Michael Wolff who read the proofs, to my mother who kept the peace, to Eva who made the tea, to Mrs Taffy Rodd and to many others whom it is impossible to mention, the compiler owes a considerable debt of gratitude. Without them this catalogue would never have been finished in the time allotted, nor would it have been successfully completed without the patient understanding of all those who own paintings by Sir Winston and whose names are recorded within it.

The theme of unselfish co-operative endeavour was already present at this catalogue's conception, for it was in someone else's evening newspaper that the compiler first read the details of Sir Winston Churchill's will. It was apparent that Sir Winston's paintings might be dispersed, and probable, therefore, that a market might develop in them; fraudulent examples might even be produced. A catalogue, made with the authority of

Sir Winston's executors, and based on those paintings still in his possession at the time of his death, would, therefore, help to establish some sort of canon of works by which others not included in it could be judged. The executors agreed with the plan.

The ideal catalogue would illustrate the paintings as far as possible in the order in which they were produced; this is convenient, orderly and purposeful in that it shows the progression of an artist's thought and technique. It also provides a morsel for the plate of the art historian, something to titillate his palate, an opportunity for more or less polite disagreement and controversy. In the event he has been served with a feast.

The pictures painted by Sir Winston while on active service during the First World War were easy to place. And so were those painted during a ministerial visit to the Near East in the early 1920s. Others had been dated with varying degrees of precision for the exhibition of some of his work in the Royal Academy in 1959, itself the climax of a world tour the previous year, when a selection had travelled across the United States, Canada, Australia and New Zealand. A number of paintings were in possession of members of his family who were able to date them as accurately as memory allowed; and a few that Sir Winston had given away elsewhere carried their dates and the circumstances of their painting with them.

1, 2, I(3), 4
79, XI(84), 110

By good fortune, those pictures whose dates were more or less accurately known were representative of several of Sir Winston's styles of painting, and the compiler was in consequence able to relate others, undated, to those which were. But not every style was represented and the situation was complicated by the evident inclination of the artist to paint in two or more different ways at roughly the same time; no doubt depending on whose painterly company he was keeping at the moment. Another complication arose from the artist's habit of putting aside canvases with which he was dissatisfied, to return to them sometimes years later; and yet another from his habit of re-working or improving pictures already finished, again with little regard to the period of their original painting.

The great variety of styles used by Sir Winston, apparent from the illustrations in this catalogue, is indicative not only of the number of painters who were his friends, but also of his sensitivity to their ideas and techniques. Sir Winston himself describes in *Painting as a Pastime*[1] how it was Lady Lavery who encouraged him to defeat his first faint-heartedness, and he later painted a series of interior scenes and portraits whose style is very close to that of Sir John Lavery himself: the self-portrait, for instance (frontispiece), which, incidentally, must surely be one of the most interesting of all the pictures in this catalogue.

[1]Odhams, 1949, Penguin, 1964

24, 26–7, III(28), 29, 31

Reference to the chapter contributed by Professor Thomas Bodkin to *Churchill by his Contemporaries*[2] will indicate the wealth of artistic ability in Sir Winston's circle, and Sir Winston's own essay on painting is valuable in this regard, albeit tangentially. There seems little point in repeating their substance here, except where it bears directly on the paintings. Some were inspired by W. R. Sickert, one directly as its title implies. Others show the influence of the work of Sir William Nicholson. Another, and a co-operative venture, bears the signatures of two other artist friends: Paul Maze and André Dunoyer de Segonzac, while Sir Winston's admiration for Daubigny and Sargent led to his copying examples of their work. And a beautiful 'Impression' of a London bridge by Monet hung in the drawing room of Chartwell, his country home in Kent and the setting for so many of his paintings. A table of knights: Sir William Orpen, Sir Oswald Birley, Sir Alfred Munnings and Sir Gerald Kelly all came within the orbit of Sir Winston's

[2]Hutchinson, 1953

155

355

162, 164–5

artistic sphere, but the most unexpected name in the group is that of Oscar Nemon the sculptor. In 1954, Sir Winston celebrated his eightieth birthday, and Mr Nemon was commissioned by Her Majesty the Queen to carve a bust of Churchill for the Royal collection. During the sittings for this Sir Winston retaliated by modelling the sculptor. For a first essay into sculpture at the age of eighty the result is certainly creditable; it is not so easy for a painter to have to think and work in three-dimensional form after a forty years' war with flat-bosomed canvas.

Throughout all his painting years Sir Winston found oil the most congenial means of expression, though he did experiment a little with tempera after the Second World War. He worked principally on canvas or canvas board, though in some cases he used panel, as in the series of studies of sea and sky. His method of working varied: at one extreme there is a painting like 'The twenty-minute sketch', which would have been produced after a long initial appraisal of the scene and without any preliminary drawing; the spontaneity and directness of this picture is obvious. At the other extreme is a painting like that of 'La Capponcina' which is relatively detailed and dependent for the accuracy of its drawing on the help of a photograph projected on to the canvas by a magic lantern. Despite this there is no hint of laboriousness or other signs of overworking – though this is apparent in other examples, the result of overmuch attention to detail. At other times again, Sir Winston would make an outline sketch in charcoal on his canvas before embarking on the actual painting; he also used this method when working directly from a snapshot or other small reminder of a favourite scene.

Many professional artists, of course, use photographs as a convenient form of quick sketch on the spot and as a preliminary to the actual execution of a picture in the studio at a later date; and the use of mechanical aids like Sir Winston's magic lantern is not so rare as some might suppose. For Sir Winston, the magic lantern and the projection of glass slides on to a canvas, were sensible methods of overcoming his lack of skill as a draughts-man, which is a necessary concomitant for success in the realistic tradition of art to which he subscribed. Not discovering painting until he was forty years old, he had no wish to waste time in learning how to draw when the effect could so easily be produced in another less laborious way. There was also the practical point that photography allowed a scene to be recorded and painted later when the rush of events precluded the completion of a satisfactory picture on the spot. The paintings of the Meuse illustrate this, for Sir Winston was actually at the scene for only one afternoon during a break in a visit to Belgium after the War. The number of variations on this picture also serves to show another facet of Sir Winston's personality as a painter: his determination to draw as much as possible from the source of his art, and to go on until he had succeeded in achieving the effect he wanted. And it was, of course, as a helpful and convenient means of achieving these ends that he justified his use of the magic lantern: if the result was the better for it, then its use was not a matter for scruples. Certainly, on the evidence, Sir Winston did not slavishly copy the photographs he used: they were merely a guide, with some details omitted, and others displaced, sometimes even to another picture.

It will be seen that there was little consistency in the way Sir Winston signed his paintings. One or two are signed in full, others were initialled only when he gave them away, regardless of when in fact they were painted, and others still from all periods of his painting career were initialled in sessions held after the war in his Studio at Chartwell. All of which goes to strengthen the usual expert distrust of signatures as any sort of guarantee

Margin references:
495–6
XVIII(104), 105–6
LVIII(391)
LXXI(475)
159
396, 400–1
LXIX(462)

of authenticity. A picture to be 'right' must be 'signed all over'; in other words it must conform in style and technique to one or more other examples known to be authentic.

Although it has been the intention of all those concerned with this catalogue that it should be comprehensive, it is recognized that it is unlikely to be finally complete, for other paintings of indisputable provenance may well turn up, either too late for inclusion or simply as a result of this book's publication. The difficulty of dating Sir Winston's pictures has led to the compiler's decision to arrange the paintings in this catalogue as far as possible in decades of work. Within this general arrangement, decade following decade, the paintings have been separated by subject and by style – a method which, if nothing else, has the advantage of making easier the discovery within these pages of works similar to those whose authenticity is in doubt, or even in the future of finding whether a genuine painting has been included or not. The dangers inherent in all this have already been displayed, for, as the manuscript goes to the publishers, new information has resulted in at least two pictures being dated some twenty years later than had been thought, but it is now impossible conveniently to adjust the catalogue order. Any corrections as to date or subject will be welcomed by the compiler; he is certainly aware of the errors, though, alas, this sense of their potential existence is clearer to him than their location or extent.

1–153
154–375
376–449
450–496

For the present therefore the catalogue must stand as it is, its compiler being already too much in debt to those who have answered his letters and borne with his questions. There are many things he would have liked to have known, but he was loath to press his inquiries further than was absolutely necessary within such a short time of Sir Winston's death. If this work has suffered thereby, it is better so.

This sense of privacy is in fact the essence of all Sir Winston's art; his pictures form a kind of pictorial diary of his quiet life: itself the nourishment of his public duties, and the haven for an often troubled mind. The paintings are therefore worthy of a more than casual glance. Apart from the many skilful still lifes, Sir Winston's paintings are principally a personal record of friends, family and household, their homes and holidays and their travels. They are the product of a man off duty, if not relaxed.

XXXII(154), 166–83
40, 42, 184
246, 318, 483

The fact that Sir Winston painted because he wanted to, and not because it was a way of making a living, leads some people to dismiss him as an amateur, with the corollary that his work cannot be taken seriously. But no one can fail to have been impressed by the bravura and distinction of Sir Winston's paintings, when examples of the best of his work have hung without embarrassment among illustrious artistic company in the London auction rooms, where there is little attempt at advantageous display or positioning. Certainly as far as his pictures are concerned, Sir Winston is the victim of his own fame as a statesman.

VII(70), 235

The light-hearted, almost flippant, tone adopted by Sir Winston in his essay *Painting as a Pastime* might well be advanced as evidence of a relatively careless attitude towards art. But facetiousness is a common shield for sensitivity, and who but a dedicated and sensitive artist could have produced the best among the works reproduced here? Enjoyment or delight are not necessarily accompanied by hilarity, and seriousness of purpose is not the same as solemnity of manner; an apparent lack of the latter does not preclude the existence of the former, it merely illustrates once again the maxim that artists should be judged largely by what they produce and not by what they say about it.

Most of the titles for the paintings that appear in this catalogue will be seen to be purely descriptive, and they can in no way be said to be inviolable or sacrosanct. Different titles for similar paintings can be explained by the fact that they belong to different people. In at least two cases, however, a title for a painting gave spark to a display of Churchillian wit.

177 That called 'Bottlescape' is so apt as to need no further comment. But 'The custody of the 491 child' is more puzzling: the larger trees obviously have a protective role; but there appears to be no reason for the hint of domestic dissension that the title conveys, until it is explained that the branches of the trees intermingle and appear to struggle together in the wind.

No one can possibly say that Sir Winston's painting is in any way an exemplar of what is called 'modern art'; but this could hardly be expected when it is recalled that he did not begin to paint seriously until he was past forty, and that this was over fifty years ago. His artist friends too were of an older era, influenced by Impressionism, but antipathetic to the formal iconoclasm of its offspring. It is only reasonable to judge a picture by its own standards and ambitions, and not by what we ourselves may find especially congenial or exciting.

When the memory of a man is still so fresh it is almost impossible to attempt any sort of unbiased assessment of his work; and the opinion of Sir Winston's friends, whatever their eminence as painters, must surely be discounted: friendship as it deepens grows blind to so many things. However, in 1925 or thereabouts, three eminent scions of the world of art sat in judgement upon an exhibition of paintings, all by amateurs, and all submitted anonymously. Each of the three, Sir Oswald Birley, Sir Kenneth Clark, and Lord Duveen, separately decided to award the first prize to what Sir Oswald later described as 'a picture of a red house in sunlight with snow on the roof, painted with great vigour'; although Lord Duveen had protested that it was surely by a professional, and 142 should be discarded. The painter was Sir Winston, and the painting is in the catalogue here.

Some twenty years later, in 1947, Sir Alfred Munnings suggested that Sir Winston submit some of his work for the judgement of those members of the Royal Academy who were selecting paintings for the annual Summer Exhibition. Sir Winston himself was very conscious of the inhibiting effect that his own fame had upon any chance of his paintings being judged on their own merits, and he insisted that they be submitted pseudonymously as by David Winter. 'I don't trust you a yard, Alfred', Munnings later reported him as saying, and in the event both pictures were accepted; one was 'Winter 142 sunshine at Chartwell' itself a seasoned warrior after its victory at the exhibition first 352 mentioned; and the other was 'The Loup River' now in the possession of the Tate Gallery, home of the national collections of British art and international modern art.

Apart from the distinction of the collections which contain examples of Sir Winston's work, his paintings have been exhibited in galleries of the standing of the Metropolitan Museum of Art in New York – only one of many famous institutions which showed examples of his work during the world tour in 1958. Following his unanimous election to membership of the Royal Academy in 1948, as its first Honorary Academician Extra-489 ordinary, Sir Winston showed paintings there regularly and by right; his Diploma Work hangs with those of the great.

The list of owners of paintings by Sir Winston reflects his own eminence; it is headed XXI(122), 434, 431 by Her Majesty the Queen, President Truman and President Eisenhower. President LIV(381) Roosevelt also owned a picture, but possession is by no means restricted to the great and indicates an almost compulsive generosity on the part of the artist. Naturally enough, the largest collection of Sir Winston's pictures is that of his wife, Lady Spencer-Churchill. In the catalogue, those given to her in his lifetime are marked simply 'Collection: Lady Spencer-Churchill'; while those still in Sir Winston's possession at the time of his death, and willed to his wife, are noted as 'The Studio, Chartwell', though of course many have since been removed from there. In the case of the other owners, and unless otherwise stated, presentation by the artist can be reasonably inferred. 298
XLV(307)
299

The colour plates that adorn this book have been specifically selected by the compiler to represent as far as possible the whole range of Sir Winston's art – his several styles and his favourite subjects. Whether or not they can be said to be a microcosm of his best work is debatable, as indeed matters of this sort are always debatable, but they have all been chosen deliberately and with no attempt to hide any of the results consequent upon ambition out-stripping technique. Questions of aesthetics are perhaps the nearest intellectual equivalent to perpetual motion. What one finds satisfying as a work of art, another, equally knowledgeable, thinks an incompetent piece of puerile nonsense. The spectrum of opinion, in fact, is as wide as the human race, and it all in the final result comes down to whether you like what you see in the light of your knowledge, experience and natural sympathies.

It may be that some will come to this book who have had little or no interest in art before, and who are attracted first by the personality and genius of Sir Winston the warrior. In fact, the most important thing about any work of art is that it is the product of a human being, of a mind which has ideas, in a body which has emotions, the whole complex, in varying proportions, finding expression on a canvas. It follows that it requires almost as much effort to appreciate a picture properly as the artist puts into producing it; and like any human product, a work of art is dependent on what has gone before, and on the circumstances, influences and limitations surrounding its production.

But there must seem only a tenuous connection between all this, and Winston Churchill in 1915, determined to subdue virgin canvas with dragon paint in the otherwise peaceful garden of Hoe Farm, Godalming. Sir Winston himself has described (in *Painting as a Pastime*) how he turned to painting as a way of distracting a mind in turmoil with ideas, but without the means of acting upon them. As a member of the Cabinet he was a party to the fateful decisions of a nation at war, but his political responsibility for the Dardanelles debacle had led to his being relieved of any executive authority. 146, 149

Successful painting requires action, organization and ideas. Execution is important, but not supremely important as it is in a work of craftsmanship; experience counts but can be gained; enthusiasm is the drive and success the spur. Sir Winston's paintings, therefore, are worth looking at because of the man who painted them, and whose ideas and emotions they express. It was a characteristically romantic gesture for Sir Winston to insist, after the Casablanca conference, that President Roosevelt accompany him to Marrakech, to see the sun set over the Atlas Mountains. The visit resulted the following day in the only picture that Churchill painted during the whole of his wartime leadership, when, for the first time perhaps, the magnitude of the task was equal to the capacity of the man. There was certainly no time for painting, nor any surplus mental energy in need of diversion. LIV(381)

Mention of this uniquely interesting picture inevitably raises the question of its monetary worth. One of the most endearingly human characteristics of the international art market is the fact that, despite all protestations to the contrary, a 'name' attached to a work of art makes a considerable difference to the price it will command. In so far as the greatest works of art have been produced by those commonly considered to be the greatest artists, this valuation on the name is a reasonable one. The method falls down however when a 'bad' picture by a 'good' artist comes up for sale, and the demand for his work among speculatively-minded collectors forces the price above what the connoisseurs reckon it to be worth. In the event both are satisfied: the collector with the knowledge that he has bought a name; and the connoisseur with the knowledge that it was not really worth it. As far as Sir Winston's pictures are concerned, like those by any artist they are in monetary terms worth at any given moment exactly, and only, what someone is prepared to pay for them.

In the ultimate, and in the context of the human situation, the worth of a work of art depends upon the worth of the person who produced it. Inspiration is the key. The inspiration engendered by great leadership is intangible but real; the inspiration contained within a work of art is also intangible and likewise real, but in so far as it is bound up with a physical object than it is, in addition, enduring – transcending death, eschewing language, subject only to decay. 'Mr Churchill wants a catalogue of his pictures made.'[1] And with all those known to have survived, this is it.

[1] From a memorandum dated 24th March, 1950

David Coombs, Godalming, 1966.

Winston Churchill 1874-1965
his paintings 1915-1958

I (3) *Plug Street 1916*

II (14) *Tapestries at Blenheim c. 1928*

III (28) *Interior of a studio, Lady Kitty Somerset at an easel c. 1922*

IV (47) *Mary's first speech c. 1929*

20

V (52) *Sunset near Roehampton c. 1919*

VI (64) *The lake at Blenheim c. 1926–9*

VII (70) *Mimizan, Landes c. 1927*

VIII (71) *Mimizan c. 1922*

24

IX (72) *Mimizan Lake c. 1922*

X (80) *View over Lympne Marshes 1925*

26

XI (84) *Cairo from the Pyramids with the artist painting 1921*

XII (87) *Pyramids and sand dunes c. 1926*

28

XIII (90) *Lake Louise, Canada c. 1929*

XIV (99) *Near Lochmore c. 1925*

XV (100) *Copy of a classical landscape c. 1925*

XVI (101) *The Papal Palace at Avignon 1925*

XVII (103) *Seascape at sunset 1920s*

XVIII (104) *Sunset over the sea – orange and purple 1920s*

XIX (112) *Storm over Cannes c. 1925*   XX (121) *The Palladian bridge at Wilton c. 1925*

34

XXI (122) *Palladian bridge c. 1925* Reproduced by gracious permission of Her Majesty the Queen

XXII (134) *Flat calm with a high-prowed boat c. 1925*

XXIII (135) *The Adriatic with Venice in the distance c. 1925*

XXIV (136) *The Firth of Forth c. 1925*

XXV (140) *Le Moulin, St-Georges-Motel c. 1923*

XXVI (141) *The entrance to a drive c. 1920*

XXVII (144) *Pergola at Chartwell c. 1925*

XXVIII (145) *Chequers on an autumn evening c. 1928*   XXIX (150) *Snow at Chartwell 1924*

XXX (151) *Lullenden Manor c. 1922*

XXXI (152) *Green trees and poppies at Lullenden c. 1920*

XXXII (154) *Magnolia c. 1930*

XXXIII (168) *A loaf of bread c. 1930*

46

XXXIV (189) *The dining-room of Sir Philip Sassoon's house, Lympne c. 1930*

XXXV (215) *View of Carcassonne, southern France c. 1930*

XXXVI (216) *The battlements at Rhodes 1930–8*

XXXVII (222) *The terrace at Lympne c.1930*   XXXVIII (232) *Château St-Georges-Motel c.1935*

50

XXXIX (256) *In the Italian garden at Hever c. 1930*

51

XL (257) *Summer house at Trent Park c. 1930*   XLI (268) *Olive trees, Cap Martin c. 1934*

52

XLII (277) *Terrace at Trent Park c. 1935*

XLIII (286) *View of Chartwell c. 1938*

54

XLIX (356) *English river landscape c. 1935*

L (358) *The Thames from Taplow c. 1935*

LI (363) *Scene on the River Loup c. 1930*

LII (365) *A lake in Norfolk c.1936*

LIII (371) *Storm scene, south of France, or, The bridge c. 1935*   LIV (381) *Tower of Katoubia Mosque 1943*

LV (382) *Buddha and lily 1948*

64

LVI (384) *Black swans at Chartwell 1948* LVII (385) *Water, Vaucluse 1948*

LVIII (391) *Sketch of Lake Carezza, or, The twenty-minute sketch 1949*

LIX (397) *Lake Geneva, Switzerland 1946*

LX (418) *Torcello 1949*

LXI (432) *Marrakech 1948*

LXII (433) *Valley of the Ourika near Marrakech 1940s*

LXIII (443) *Le Béguinage, Bruges 1946*

LXIV (445) *View from Chartwell c. 1948*

LXV (446) *Chartwell kitchen garden 1948*

LXVI (455) *Oranges and lemons 1958*

LXVII (456) *Lady Churchill at the launching of HMS Indomitable c. 1954*

LXVIII (461) *The marble staircase at Hatfield c. 1951*

LXIX (462) *Gate at Marrakech, a man on a donkey c. 1950*

LXX (473) *Cap d'Ail 1952*

LXXI (475) *The walled garden at Capponcina c. 1955*

LXXII (494) *View of Menton and Italy from La Pausa 1957*

THE PAINTINGS
a background sketch

[1]WINSTON S. CHURCHILL, Heinemann, 1966

The purpose of these notes is to provide some sort of outline background to the paintings of Sir Winston Churchill. It is little more than a sketch. Not until the completion of Mr Randolph Churchill's official biography[1] will the canvas be properly filled with the persons and places that the pictures and their owners evoke. In harmony too with the essentially arbitrary arrangement of the catalogue, this account is chronological only in the widest sense.

Introduction, *page* 14

146, 149

It was at Hoe Farm in 1915 that Sir Winston first found the opportunity as well as the inspiration to paint. The Churchills rented the house for several months, and one of the pictures painted there includes the figure of Lady Gwendeline Churchill, Sir Winston's sister-in-law, who with her husband and family were frequent guests then as elsewhere in later years.

The move from the post of First Lord of the Admiralty to that of Chancellor of the Duchy of Lancaster in May 1915 was the impetus for Sir Winston's painting career. Politically it was a change from activity to passivity, and in six months or so he resigned from the government to go to the front. Churchill was, of course, no stranger to active service, and went to France to serve as a major with the Grenadier Guards. He was promoted to lieutenant-colonel and given command of the Sixth Battalion of the Royal Scots Fusiliers. His regimental headquarters were at Lawrence Farm near Ploegsteert, the latter name giving the British an excellent opportunity for showing their sturdy and unfailing disregard of foreign pronunciation, and 'Plug Street' it inevitably became.

1, 2, I(3), 4

Sir Winston's second-in-command was Major Sir Archibald Sinclair (later Lord Thurso) and it is he who sits behind a newspaper in several of the series of wartime paintings.

Late in 1916 Churchill's battalion was absorbed. He had been promised a brigade by

48

General Sir John French though, with the latter's unforeseen recall, the opportunity was lost, and Churchill decided to return to politics. The next year saw his public vindication by the report of the commission that had investigated the Dardanelles campaign, and a new prime minister, Lloyd George, eventually made him Minister of Munitions. The commander of the land forces at the Dardanelles had been General Sir Ian Hamilton, an old friend of Churchill's from Indian and South African campaigns, and the eventual

235

owner of one of Sir Winston's finest paintings, that of Ightham Mote.

In 1918 Churchill's considerable gifts for organization were further recognized by his being made responsible for the task of demobilization as Secretary of State for War and Air. For three years his energies were in this way absorbed, though some reminders of

51

relaxation remain in the painting of Loch Choire on the Duke of Sutherland's Scottish

50, V(52)

estate and in the pictures painted when he was staying at Templeton with his cousins, the Guests, to play on the nearby Roehampton polo-ground.

In 1921 the consequences of the First World War, and, in particular, Turkey's involvement in it with Germany, began directly to affect the countries of the Eastern

Mediterranean. The task of dealing with the situation came to Churchill's hand. He was transferred to the Colonial Office. He simplified the administrative responsibilities for the area and faced the complicated claims of nationalism with the aid, amongst others, of the already legendary Lawrence of Arabia. Preferring always to see things for himself, Churchill took the opportunity now of travelling to the Middle East. He painted at Jerusalem, and at Cairo, where he presided at the conference that settled for a while the racial and tribal disputes. *110, 79, XI(84)*

As the many canvases show, Sir Winston often painted in North Africa, particularly later on Marrakech. These Moroccan pictures are a reminder of his friendship with the painter Sir John Lavery, who had a house in Tangier, and whose strong influence is clear in many early pictures. Sir John was one of the most successful artists of his time, his London studio being the resort of society as well as a whirlwind of politics, for Sir John and his wife were both ardent supporters of an independent Ireland. This was an ancient concept that finally erupted into internal war, Sir Winston being in the forefront of those who helped it to an honourable conclusion, as Michael Collins, the tragic Irish patriot, himself affirmed. *81, 214, LXII(433)* *24*

Mention of Lady Lavery recalls Sir Winston's fair rescuer from an early painterly defeat. Another visitor to the scene of Churchill's first months of trial and inspiration had been Sir Edward Marsh, for many ministerial years his chief Civil Service aide and Private Secretary. This remarkable man was the patron and anthologist of the Georgian poets, being impressed particularly by the verse of Rupert Brooke. He was also a connoisseur of painting in which respect he was a continuing influence on Sir Winston's work, being a constant visitor to Chartwell between the two world wars. Sir Edward became a Trustee of the National and Tate Galleries, and in his later years Chairman of the Contemporary Art Society, whose collective resources go to the purchase for British public galleries of significant examples of modern art. *Introduction, page 14*

Several of Sir Winston's paintings have poetic connections, with that set in Newbuildings a specific one. This was the house of Wilfrid Scawen Blunt, remembered today for his poetry, by some for his love of the desert, and some few even may recall his parliamentary career; certainly, his house was often the setting for those gatherings of the political and the artistic whose lively and provocative company Sir Winston so often enjoyed. Knebworth House recalls Sir Winston's life-long friendship with Lord and Lady Lytton; the latter, before her marriage the beautiful Miss Pamela Plowden, has been described by Mr Randolph Churchill, in his biography, as the first great love of Sir Winston's life. Her husband, the second Earl, was the grandson of Bulwer-Lytton, the novelist, and son of the first Earl who wrote as the poet Owen Meredith. Lord Lytton combined an interest in the arts, particularly the theatre, with unorthodox political opinions which included strong and early support of the suffragettes. In the painting that Sir Winston later gave to Lady Juliet Duff there is yet another poetic connection, for she was the Juliet whom Hilaire Belloc addressed in verse, and whose patronage encouraged so many young aspirants to the arts. *16* *10, 22* *56*

The peaceful landscape of Norfolk spreads through several of Sir Winston's pictures, some of which are set in the vicinity of Breccles Hall, owned by Edwin Montagu, whose wife, the brilliant and amusing Venetia Stanley, was a cousin of Sir Winston's wife. Montagu himself took a particular delight in shooting and also had an ardent enough interest in natural history to establish a bird sanctuary in company with Lord Grey of *LII(365)* *186, 260*

Falloden, the naturalist and one-time Foreign Secretary. As a politician, Montagu was particularly concerned with constitutional reform in India, and in 1922 he resigned as Secretary of State for India which contributed to the eventual break-up of the old wartime coalition. Parliament was dissolved, and in the election which followed Churchill was defeated after having sat continuously in the House of Commons since 1900.

[1]WORLD CRISIS, 6 Vols. Thornton, Butterworth, 1923–31; 4 Vols. Four Square, 1960

143, XXX(151), XXXI(152)

The following year saw the publication of the first part of Churchill's history of the First World War[1]. It was immensely successful, and an unexpected legacy enabled Churchill to think about buying a country house for his wife and family. The paintings at Lullenden Manor are reminders of an earlier temporary home, but it was with the beautiful setting of Chartwell near Westerham in the same county of Kent that Sir Winston fell finally in love.

XLIII(286), LXIV(287), 375

344, 482

LXV(446), IV(47)

Many paintings tell the long story of Churchill's devotion to this place. They show the lovely valley and the distant view from the house high on one hill, the swimming pool, the lakes, and many other watery delights planned and constructed by Sir Winston, as well as the long kitchen garden wall he built so laboriously and expertly, with intermittent family aid.

36

To Chartwell came a host of friends and a few may be seen in one of the paintings of a Churchill family tea: Edward Marsh already mentioned, Professor Lindemann (later Lord Cherwell), Churchill's scientific adviser during the Second World War, and the English painter W. R. Sickert. In Sickert there was a link with the French Impressionists, for Degas was his master, and Renoir, Monet and Pissarro his friends; his wife Thérèse was the daughter of the painter Jules Lessore.

The dining-room was also the setting for a large oil sketch by another painter friend showing Sir Winston and Lady Churchill at breakfast. The artist was Sir William Nicholson, and his picture still hangs at Chartwell in that very room. Sir William Nicholson was a much loved friend of both Sir Winston and Lady Churchill; he often visited Chartwell and frequently painted there with Sir Winston, on whom he had a great artistic influence. Nicholson himself was one of the many who owed much to the early encouragement of the great American-Parisian painter, James Abbot McNeill Whistler.

XXXIV(189), XXXVII(222)

20, XLII(277)

Another Kentish house that appears in many of Sir Winston's pictures is Port Lympne which, with Trent Park, formed a brace of country homes for Sir Philip Sassoon, a politician and connoisseur who was responsible, among other things, for the restoration of Sir James Thornhill's Painted Hall at Greenwich. His London house in Park Lane saw many charity exhibitions of paintings, furniture, porcelain and silver, as well as a celebrated series of weekly political luncheons, while Lympne itself was a favourite meeting place for the politicians involved in the lengthy processes of the Peace Conference at Versailles.

Also present at Versailles was Sir William Orpen in the capacity of an official war artist, although he was better known in his day as a society portrait painter, whose sitters had included Sir Winston himself. It was Orpen who had told Churchill of Avignon's light, and two pictures commemorate the subsequent visit. Monet was the prime apostle of the complexities of light (one of his London river paintings was given later to Sir Winston) and among Monet's most fervent admirers was yet another portrait painter, the American J. S. Sargent, who inhabited Whistler's London studio in Tite Street, Chelsea. Sargent's work was itself greatly admired by Churchill, who showed an early and typically independent appreciation of his landscapes; he even copied one that belonged to Sir Philip Sassoon.

94, XVI(101)

179, 116, 440

With the Chartwell adventure begun, in 1924 Sir Winston was re-elected to Parliament. He had changed his party, if not his opinions, for the second time; indeed it might be said with more truth that, following the tortuous evolutionary path of politics, his party had returned to him. The Prime Minister appointed him Chancellor of the Exchequer (the position from which his father had disastrously once resigned), and the introduction of widows' pensions in his first budget was an echo of some of Churchill's earlier social reforms.

In 1926 there was the General Strike, and Churchill returned to journalism in command of an improvised daily newspaper named *The British Gazette*, which had a wide circulation with exclusive government support. This short period of furious activity was followed by a painting holiday abroad, when the Pyramids, the Parthenon and the Forum XII(87), 97, 95 fell successively to his brush.

The general election of 1929 gave Britain her second Socialist government and, although turned out of office, Sir Winston this time managed to retain his parliamentary seat. He visited Canada, where he painted in the Rockies on Lake Louise and later stayed XIII(90), 91 in California with the newspaper magnate and compulsive collector of art and antiques, William Randolph Hearst. In the particular context of his paintings, three British newspaper proprietors are also to be found amongst Sir Winston's friends: Lord Camrose at Hackwood Park, Lord Astor at Hever Castle near Chartwell, which was obviously a 75, XXXIX(256) source of much inspiration to the artist, and finally, Lord Beaverbrook, whose villa, La Capponcina on the French Riviera at Cap d'Ail, saw Sir Winston often as a visitor in LXX(473) his later years.

Apart from the many paintings on and around the Riviera, Sir Winston was responsible XXXV(215), XLVI(309), LI(363) for a fine series of pictures at Mimizan, sixty miles from Bordeaux, where the Duke of 63, 65–7, IX(72) Westminster had a house and his old Prime Minister, Lloyd George, was given one of the VII(70) best of these. Churchill also painted at others of the Duke's properties: Eaton Hall near 255 Chester, and Lochmore in the Scottish highlands. XIV(99), 192–5

The advent of the next decade, which was to find Churchill politically isolated, and his own repeated warnings scorned or ignored, saw, almost symbolically, the deaths of two friends from his earliest political days; first, F. E. Smith, Lord Birkenhead, brilliant advocate and forceful politician, two of whose family are seen in the paintings here, and 18, 227 second, A. J. Balfour, first Earl, who, in 1902, had succeeded his uncle, the Marquess of 32–3 Salisbury, as Prime Minister. The epitome of the philosopher statesman, Balfour had later served Lloyd George as Foreign Secretary during the latter part of the First World War, and at Versailles. His innate humanity and wisdom led him alike to promote the idea of a Palestine shared and settled by both Arabs and Jews, as he also sought to avoid Germany's humiliation after the war. Another man who strove to revive the beaten spirit of Germany, so that she could take her necessary place in the life of the world, was Viscount d'Abernon who lived at Esher Place. He was Britain's first post-war Ambassador 137 to Germany, until 1926. Here, too, we have another connection with art, for Lord d'Abernon was later a Trustee of the National Gallery and the Tate Gallery.

For Churchill the 1930s, if barren politically, at least gave him the opportunity to embark upon and complete a monumental biography of his illustrious ancestor, the first Duke of Marlborough[1]. This act of literary homage is commemorated in the paintings of [1]MARLBOROUGH, HIS LIFE AND TIMES, 4 Vols., Harrap, 1933–8 the Marlborough tapestries at Blenheim, the grand setting for Sir Winston's own birth six decades before. In these years Churchill also travelled a great deal, several times 11–13, II(14), 59–61, VI(64)

XLVIII(345) visiting the United States on lecture tours. There he met Albert Einstein, whose theory of relativity had transformed the scientific world, and in New York found a memory of the Mississippi novelist, Mark Twain, who, in 1900, had chaired a meeting addressed by Churchill on his Boer War escapades. Of his European visits, the holidays are principally 267, XLI(268) recorded in Sir Winston's paintings at the lovely Riviera villa, La Dragonnière, now 230–1, XXXVIII(232), 233–4 owned by Count and Countess d'Estainville, and in those at St-Georges-Motel, a French château belonging to Mme. Consuelo Vanderbilt Balsan, the first wife of Churchill's X(80), XXVI(141), XLIX(356), (L358) cousin, the ninth Duke of Marlborough. These were productive decades for painting in England too.

In 1936 it looked as if Churchill's view of the dangers inherent in the European scene would come to be accepted, for the occupation of the Rhineland and the subjugation of Abyssinia forced an unhappy admission from the Prime Minister of the time. But the tide of public opinion swiftly turned against Churchill again when he loyally and publicly supported the new king in the crisis that led to the latter's abdication. Three more years rolled and war came. In 1939 Churchill returned to head the Board of Admiralty, the XXIV(316) very same position from which he had been so unceremoniously sacked a quarter of a century before. And then the painting had to stop.

Prime Minister in 1940, Winston Churchill went to war for his Sovereign, hurled Introduction, *page* 14 defiance in the face of defeat, and won victory in the end through a Grand Alliance. He LIV(381) found only one opportunity to paint in the whole course of the War.

Electoral dismissal in 1945, ungrateful though it may have seemed on the part of a nation who owed him so much, nevertheless left Churchill untrammelled with the details of domestic social and economic revolution, so that his words, with their unique prestige, went instead to rebuild the self-confidence of the world. From his initial dejection by 383 Lake Como in 1945, Sir Winston travelled to be acclaimed in Europe and the United 422, LIX(397) States. Speeches in 1946 at Fulton and Zurich were visionary in conception and creative in act, seeking to bring the United States to Britain and so to Europe, and France and Germany together for the peace of all. Churchill himself came of an Anglo-American union, and in 1963 was given the unique privilege of an Honorary Citizenship of the United States. Though too much should not be made of it, most of Churchill's paintings were, in his post-war years, of scenes abroad.

379, LVI(384) The painting of his beloved black swans at Chartwell brings us back to England and 377, LV(382) the monumental Buddha and brilliant lilies mark a return of interest in the close-bound subtleties of the traditional still life. Churchill's sense of adventure still remained keen, for he experimented vigorously with tempera at this time as a change from his more usual oils. One of Sir Winston's most charming portraits also dates from these years, 380 that of one of his secretaries. The additional initials 'O.B.' refer to the presence during the sitting of Sir Oswald Birley, the portrait painter; a friendship which is also com-XX(121), XXI(122) memorated in the earlier pictures of the Palladian Bridge at Wilton, ancient seat of the Earls of Pembroke, where Sir Winston and Sir Oswald had often been guests and painted together. The years between 1946 and 1951, when Churchill became Prime Minister XXVIII(145) again (and the picture of Chequers, the official country residence of Britain's premiers, is a reminder of this, however out of time) marked the publication of the first volumes of his history of the Second World War. Some of his more venerable paintings were also rescued at this time: the copy of a classical landscape, for instance, was found folded and XV(100) forgotten under a bench in his studio, as the oblique mark across it testifies.

The death of King George VI in 1952 moved Churchill to a grand panegyric, though he turned immediately to support and serve the new young Queen. Resigning finally as Prime Minister in 1955, Sir Winston occupied himself with the completion and publication of his wise and compelling *History of the English Speaking Peoples*[1]. In the following year, Churchill received at Aachen the first Charlemagne prize, using the occasion to broadcast his view of Russia as an integral part of Europe – an unpopular opinion then, and to be realised still.

[1]Cassell, 1956–8

His last paintings were done principally at Marrakech, and at La Capponcina, Lord Beaverbrook's villa on Cap d'Ail; and finally among the stimulating company of a superb collection of Impressionist works at La Pausa, the Riviera villa of Mr Emery Reves, an old friend and supporter of his supra-national ideals.

467, LXXI(475)

LXVI(455), LXXII(494)

D.C.

Reproductions in monochrome
with catalogue entries of all the
paintings illustrated in this book.

Note In the captions, the owners' names are listed in chronological order, the last named being the owner at the time this catalogue was compiled.

1 *Plug Street, Lawrence Farm 1916*
18 × 24 in.
Initialled
COLLECTION : Lord Thurso

2 *Plug Street, Battalion Headquarters 1916*
10 × 14 in. Oil on board
Initialled
COLLECTIONS : 6th Battalion, The Royal Scots Fusiliers
Trustees of the Divisional Funds of the
9th Scottish Division
The Board of Her Majesty's Commissioners
for Queen Victoria School

I (3) *Plug Street 1916*
20 × 24 in.
Initialled
EXHIBITIONS : World Tour 1958
Royal Academy 1959
New York World's Fair 1965
COLLECTION : Mr Randolph Churchill

4

5

6

7

8

4 *Plug Street 1916*
  20 × 24 in.
  Initialled
  EXHIBITIONS: World Tour 1958
  Royal Academy 1959
  New York World's Fair 1965
  COLLECTION: Lady Spencer-Churchill

5 *Flowers in a green-glass vase c. 1925*
  36 × 24 in.
  Unsigned
  The Studio, Chartwell

6 *Roses c. 1928*
  20 × 14 in. Canvas on hardboard
  Initialled
  COLLECTION: Lady Spencer-Churchill

7 *Mallows c. 1928*
  23½ × 19½ in.
  Initialled
  The Studio, Chartwell

8 *Flowers, painted in the Studio at Chartwell c. 1928*
  24 × 20 in.
Initialled
ILLUSTRATED: *Painting as a Pastime*
EXHIBITIONS: World Tour 1958
Royal Academy 1959
COLLECTION: Lady Spencer-Churchill

9 *Fruit and two jars c. 1920*
  27 × 32 in.
Initialled
COLLECTION: Lady Spencer-Churchill

10 *The Banqueting Hall, Knebworth House 1920s*
   23 × 36 in.
   Initialled
   COLLECTION : Lady Lytton

11 *Tapestries at Blenheim c. 1930*
   25 × 30 in.
   Initialled
   ILLUSTRATED : *Painting as a Pastime*
   EXHIBITIONS : Royal Academy 1948
   World Tour 1958
   Royal Academy 1959
   COLLECTION : Mrs Christopher Soames

12 *State Room at Blenheim c. 1928*
   20 × 24 in.
   Initialled
   EXHIBITION : New York World's Fair 1965
   COLLECTION : Mr Joyce C. Hall

13 *Great Hall, Blenheim c. 1928*
30 × 25 in.
Unsigned
COLLECTION : Duke of Marlborough

II (14) *Tapestries at Blenheim c. 1928*
24½ × 30 in.
Unsigned
COLLECTION : Mr Randolph Churchill

15

16

17

18

15 *Pedimented doorway c. 1922*
   20 × 14 in. Canvas board
   Unsigned
   The Studio, Chartwell

16 *The hallway of Wilfrid Scawen Blunt's home :
   Newbuildings, Sussex c. 1920*
   24 × 20 in.
   Initialled
   The Studio, Chartwell

17 *A music room c. 1928*
   17 × 10½ in.
   Unsigned
   The Studio, Chartwell

18 *The living-room at Lympne with Lady Pamela Smith c. 1925*
20 × 24 in.
Unsigned
The Studio, Chartwell

19 *The library of Sir Philip Sassoon's house at Lympne c. 1928*
24 × 20 in.
Initialled
The Studio, Chartwell

20 *The Blue Room, Trent Park 1934*
   $19\frac{1}{2} \times 13\frac{1}{2}$ in. Canvas board
   Initialled and dated
   ILLUSTRATED: *Painting as a Pastime*
   EXHIBITION: Royal Academy 1948
   COLLECTIONS: (Christie's Charity Sale 1949)
   Mr Guerios
   Museo de Arte, São Paulo, Brazil

21 *The Blue Room, Trent Park c. 1920*
   20×14 in. Canvas board
   Unsigned
   The Studio, Chartwell

22 *The dining-room at Knebworth c. 1928*
   20×14 in.
   Unsigned
   The Studio, Chartwell

23 *The inner hall at Breccles c. 1928*
16 × 22 in.
Initialled
The Studio, Chartwell

24 *The interior of Sir John Lavery's studio, with*
   Lady Lavery and another at their easels c. 1922
   24 × 20 in.
   Initialled
   COLLECTION: Lady Spencer–Churchill

25 *A long gallery with oak furniture c. 1928*
   20 × 24 in.
   Initialled
   The Studio, Chartwell

 26

27

26 *The interior of Sir John Lavery's*
  studio with two ladies c. 1922
  Pencil sketch on back 18 × 12 in. Canvas board
  Unsigned
  The Studio, Chartwell

27 *Studio sketch*
  (*Sir John Lavery's*) *c. 1920*
  20 × 24 in.
  Initialled
  COLLECTION : Lady Spencer-Churchill

III (28) *Interior of a studio,*
  Lady Kitty Somerset at an easel c. 1922
  27 × 20 in.
  Initialled
  COLLECTION : Lady Spencer-Churchill

29a

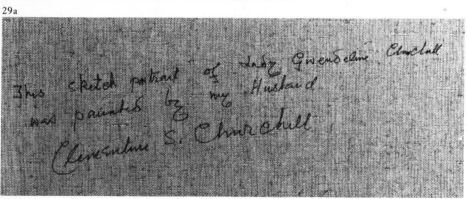

29 *Portrait of Lady Gwendeline Churchill c. 1920*
   30 × 25 in.
   Unsigned
   Inscribed on the back : 'Painted by my husband. Clementine S. Churchill' Relined and
   subsequently inscribed : 'This sketch portrait of Lady Gwendeline Churchill was painted by my
   Husband. Clementine S. Churchill' (*see* 29a)
   The Studio, Chartwell
   COLLECTION : Mr Peregrine Churchill

30

30 *Portrait of Lady Lavery 1920s*
30 × 25 in.
Unsigned
The Studio, Chartwell

frontispiece (31) *Self-portrait c. 1920*
24 × 20 in.
Unsigned
Inscribed on the back:
'Self portrait, painted by my husband.
Clementine S. Churchill'
The Studio, Chartwell

32 *Lord Balfour and his niece on a log 1920s*
   20 × 24 ins.
   Unsigned
   Inscribed on the back:
   'Painted by my husband. Clementine S. Churchill'
   The Studio, Chartwell

33 *Lord Balfour 1920s*
   20 × 16 in.
   Unsigned
   The Studio, Chartwell
   COLLECTION: Marquess of Salisbury

34 *Mme Chanel with a dachshund c. 1928*
   17½ × 14 in. Board
   Unsigned
   The Studio, Chartwell

35 *The guardsman 1920s*
  20 × 12 in.
  Initialled
  On Sentry Go – in the snow at Buckingham Palace
  COLLECTION : Mr Giovanni Agnelli

36 *Tea at Chartwell c. 1928*
  25 × 30 in.
  Unsigned
  The dining-room, 29th August 1927. Mrs Thérèse Sickert,
  Diana Mitford, Edward Marsh, Winston Churchill,
  Professor Lindemann, Randolph Churchill,
  Diana Churchill, Mrs Churchill, Richard Sickert.
  From a photograph taken by Donald Ferguson.
  The Studio, Chartwell

37

38

39

37 *Sir Archibald Sinclair (Lord Thurso) 1920s*
   30 × 25 in.
   Unsigned
   The Studio, Chartwell

38 *Mr Jack Scott c. 1925*
   24 × 20 in.
   Unsigned
   The Studio, Chartwell

39 *The parrot 1920s*
   20 × 14 in.
   Unsigned
   The Studio, Chartwell

40 *Lord Darling c. 1925*
30 × 25 in.
Unsigned
The Studio, Chartwell

41 *Children laughing 1920s*
14 × 20 in. Canvas board
Initialled
Punch and Judy. A London street study.
The Studio, Chartwell

42 *Teatime in the loggia at Chartwell – with
Miss Marryott Whyte, Mrs Churchill,
Diana and Mary c. 1928*
16 × 24 in.
Initialled
The Studio, Chartwell

43 *Sir Winston Churchill painting under the
loggia at Chartwell 1927*
20 × 14 in. Board
Unsigned
The Studio, Chartwell

44 *Two ladies in a gondola on the lagoon at*
   Venice c. 1925
   20 × 14 in. Canvas board
   Unsigned
   The Studio, Chartwell

45 *Hunting scene c. 1928*
   20 × 16 in.
   Unsigned
   COLLECTIONS: Lady Spencer-Churchill
   Miss Emma Soames

46 *Still life: Randolph Churchill under*
   the pergola at Chartwell 1920s
   24 × 20 in.
   Unsigned
   The Studio, Chartwell

48

49

50

IV (47) *Mary's first speech c. 1929*
15 × 21 in.
Unsigned
COLLECTION : Mrs Christopher Soames

48 *Troops going to the Front 1920s*
20 × 24 in.
Unsigned
Victoria Station, London, 1917.
COLLECTION : Lord Butler

49 *The fire c. 1928*
28 × 36 in.
Unsigned
Three fire brigades were called to a
bus garage in Bures, Suffolk.
The Studio, Chartwell

50 *Sunset at Roehampton, or,*
Sunset through fog 1919
24 × 20 in.
Initialled
EXHIBITIONS: World Tour 1958
Royal Academy 1959
COLLECTION: Lady Spencer-Churchill

51 *Loch Choire, Scotland, August 1919*
17½ × 13½ in. Canvas on board
Initialled
EXHIBITIONS: Royal Academy 1959
New York World's Fair 1965
COLLECTIONS: Duke of Sutherland
Clare, Duchess of Sutherland
Sold Parke-Bernet 19th May 1966

V (52) *Sunset near Roehampton c. 1919*
24 × 20 in.
Initialled
COLLECTION: Sarah, Lady Audley

53

54

55

56

53 *Woods at Mimizan, Landes c. 1924*
30 × 25 in.
Initialled
EXHIBITIONS : World Tour 1958
Royal Academy 1959
COLLECTION : Mr Edward Heath

54 *Garden scene at Breccles c. 1925*
18 × 24 in.
Initialled
The Studio, Chartwell

55 *Large cedar in the formal
garden at Breccles 1920s*
24 × 20 in.
Unsigned
The Studio, Chartwell

56 *The Thames at Taplow 1920s*
25 × 30 in.
Initialled
COLLECTION : The late Lady Juliet Duff
Sold by the legatee, Parke–Bernet 20th October 1966.

57 *Winter woodland, Breccles c. 1925*
20 × 16 in.
Initialled
EXHIBITION : Royal Academy 1959
COLLECTION : Dame Pattie Menzies

58 *Quiet waters 1920s* (*?*)
20 × 24 in.
Unsigned
COLLECTIONS: Lord Beaverbrook
(Presented by the artist May 1959
on occasion of the recipient's 80th birthday)
Beaverbrook Art Gallery

59 *Cannon Point, Blenheim Lake 1920s*
26 × 31 in.
Initialled
COLLECTION: Duke of Marlborough

60 *Wooded water near Blenheim 1920s*
32 × 23 in.
Initialled
COLLECTION: Mr Anthony Montague Browne

61 *Boathouse,*
   Blenheim Lake 1920s
   28 × 25 in.
   Unsigned
   COLLECTION:
   Duke of Marlborough

62 *Mimizan 1920s*
   21½ × 13½ in.
   Initialled
   COLLECTION:
   Field Marshal Viscount Montgomery

63 *Evening glow at Mimizan 1920s*
   20 × 24 in.
   Initialled
   EXHIBITION:
   New York World's Fair 1965
   COLLECTIONS:
   Mrs Diana Sandys
   Mrs Piers Dixon

VI (64) *The lake at Blenheim c. 1926–9*
   20 × 24 in.
   Signed and initialled
   COLLECTIONS:
   Field Marshal Viscount Montgomery
   Sold Parke-Bernet, 19th May 1966

65

66

67

68

65 *Woodland scene near Mimizan 1920s*
24 × 20 in.
Initialled
EXHIBITION: New York World's Fair 1965
COLLECTION: Mr J. R. Colville

66 *Trees, Mimizan c. 1925*
24 × 20 in.
Unsigned
EXHIBITION:
Royal Academy 1959
COLLECTION:
Lady Spencer-Churchill

67 *Red-roofed house at Mimizan 1920s*
24 × 20 in.
Initialled
COLLECTIONS:
Lady Spencer-Churchill
Mr E. Murray

68 *Trees by a stream in Norfolk
c. 1923*
24 × 20 in.
Unsigned
COLLECTION:
Lady Spencer-Churchill

69 *Mimizan 1924*
 30 × 25 in.
 Initialled
 EXHIBITIONS:
 World Tour 1958
 Royal Academy 1959
 COLLECTION:
 Lady Spencer-Churchill

VII (70) *Mimizan, Landes c. 1927*
 $24\frac{1}{2}$ × $29\frac{1}{2}$ in.
 Initialled
 COLLECTIONS:
 Mr David Lloyd George
 Viscount Tenby
 Sold Christie's, 12th November 1965

VIII (71) *Mimizan c. 1922*
 24 × 20 in.
 Initialled
 COLLECTIONS:
 Lady Spencer-Churchill
 Mrs Piers Dixon

IX (72) *Mimizan Lake c. 1922*
 24 × 20 in.
 Initialled
 EXHIBITIONS:
 World Tour 1958
 Royal Academy 1959
 COLLECTIONS:
 Lady Spencer-Churchill
 Government Whips' Office

73 *View of Cherkley 1915(?)*
20 × 23 in.
Initialled
COLLECTIONS:
Lord Beaverbrook
Beaverbrook Art Gallery

74 *Cork trees near Mimizan 1924*
26 × 30 in. Signed
EXHIBITIONS: World Tour 1958
Royal Academy 1959
New York World's Fair 1965
COLLECTIONS: Lady Spencer-Churchill
Sotheby's Charity Auction 1961
(World Refugee Year)
Mr Sigurd S. Larmon

75 *Hackwood Park 1920s*
32 × 26 in.
Initialled
COLLECTION:
Viscount Camrose

76 *Garden scene 1920s*
28 × 24 in.
Initialled
COLLECTION: Lady Lytto

77

78

79

77 *The fountain in the shade c. 1925*
  24 × 20 in.
  Initialled
  COLLECTION:
  Lady Spencer-Churchill

78 *Trent Park c. 1925*
  20 × 14 in.
  Canvas board
  Unsigned
  The Studio, Chartwell

79 *Cairo from the Pyramids 1921*
  25 × 30 in.
  Initialled
  EXHIBITION:
  Royal Academy 1959
  COLLECTIONS:
  Lady Spencer-Churchill
  Duke of Norfolk

X (80) *View over Lympne Marshes 1925*
  20 × 24½ in.
  Unsigned
  COLLECTION:
  Mr Randolph Churchill

81

81 *Marrakech c. 1935*
14 × 20 in. Canvas board
Unsigned
The Studio, Chartwell

82 *Distant view of the*
Pyramids at sunset c. 1926
25 × 30 in.
Unsigned
The Studio, Chartwell

83 *The entrance of the Gorge*
at Todhra c. 1935
14 × 20 in. Canvas board
Unsigned
COLLECTION:
Lady Spencer-Churchill

XI (84) *Cairo from the Pyramids*
with the artist painting c. 1921
40 × 50 in.
Unsigned
COLLECTION:
Lady Spencer-Churchill

85

86

85 *Distant view of the Pyramids c. 1926*
25 × 30 in.
Unsigned
The Studio, Chartwell

86 *The Pyramids c. 1921*
25 × 30 in.
Unsigned
The Studio, Chartwell

XII (87) *Pyramids and sand dunes c. 1926*
25 × 30 in.
Unsigned
The Studio, Chartwell

88 *Coast scene with a ruined building c. 1920*
  20 × 24 in.
  Unsigned
  The Studio, Chartwell

89 *In the Dolomites c. 1925*
  14 × 20 in. Canvas board
  Unsigned
  The Studio, Chartwell

XIII (90) *Lake Louise, Canada c. 1929*
  24 × 32 in.
  Unsigned
  The Studio, Chartwell

91 *Lake Louise, Canada c. 1929*
14 × 20 in. Canvas board
Unsigned
The Studio, Chartwell

92 *Lake scene in the Dolomites c. 1925*
18 × 26 in.
Unsigned
The Studio, Chartwell

93 *Coast scene in the south of France, with a cactus c. 1925*
20 × 24 in.
Unsigned
The Studio, Chartwell

94

95

96

97

94 *Avignon 1925*
    19 × 29 in.
    Initialled
    EXHIBITIONS:
    World Tour 1958
    Royal Academy 1959
    COLLECTIONS:
    Mr Winston Churchill
    Lady Spencer-Churchill

95 *The Forum in Rome c. 1926*
    20 × 14 in. Canvas board
    Unsigned
    The Studio, Chartwell

96 *Coast near Cannes 1925*
    20 × 28 in.
    Unsigned
    The Studio, Chartwell

97 *Ruined Greek temple c. 1925*
    20 × 14 in. Canvas board
    Unsigned
    The Studio, Chartwell

98 *Calm sea near Marseilles*
c. 1926
13 × 16 in. Panel
Unsigned
The Studio, Chartwell

XIV (99) *Near Lochmore c. 1925*
25 × 30 in.
Unsigned
The Studio, Chartwell

XV (100) *Copy of a classical landscape*
c. 1925
25 × 30 in.
Initialled
The Studio, Chartwell

XVI (101) *The Papal Palace at Avignon 1925*
24 × 36 in.
Unsigned
COLLECTION:
Mr Randolph Churchill

102 *East coast landscape 1920s*
25 × 30 in.
Unsigned
The Studio, Chartwell

XVII (103) *Seascape at sunset 1920s*
18 × 36 in.
Initialled
COLLECTION: Lady Spencer-Churchill

XVIII (104) *Sunset over the sea – orange and purple 1920s*
13 × 16 in. Panel
Unsigned
The Studio, Chartwell

105 *Seascape with rain clouds c. 1928*
13 × 16 in. Panel
Unsigned
The Studio, Chartwell

106 *Sunset over the sea –
pink and mauve 1920s*
13 × 16 in. Panel
Unsigned
The Studio, Chartwell

107 *Seascape with a conical buoy c. 1928*
20 × 24 in.
Initialled
The Studio, Chartwell

108 *Purple mountains and a blue
sea at sunset c. 1928*
13 × 16 in. Panel
Unsigned
The Studio, Chartwell

109 *Impression of a cloud-swept landscape in the south of France 1920s*
13 × 16 in. Panel
Unsigned
The Studio, Chartwell

110 *Jerusalem 1921*
20 × 24 in.
Initialled
EXHIBITIONS:
World Tour 1958
Royal Academy 1959
COLLECTION: Lady Spencer-Churchill

111 *Coastal town on the Riviera c. 1925*
Sketch of a lady on back
14 × 20 in. Canvas board
Unsigned
The Studio, Chartwell

113 114

115

XIX (112) *Storm over Cannes c. 1925*
    20 × 24 in.
    Unsigned
    The Studio, Chartwell

113 *Remains of Greek temple,*
    doorway and pillars c. 1926
    20 × 14 in. Canvas board
    Unsigned
    The Studio, Chartwell

114 *Doorway and pillars*
    in shadow c. 1926
    20 × 14 in. Canvas board
    Unsigned
    The Studio, Chartwell

115 *Pillars of a ruined temple c. 1926*
    14 × 20 in. Canvas board
    Unsigned
    The Studio, Chartwell

116 *Ruins of Amiens Cathedral*
  (*after a Sargent in the*
  possession of Sir Philip Sassoon) *1920s*
  23 × 29 in.
  Unsigned
  COLLECTION: Mr Randolph Churchill

117 *The Palladian bridge at Wilton*
  c. 1925
  Unfinished
  14 × 19¾ in. Canvas board.
  Unsigned
  The Studio, Chartwell

118 *The Palladian bridge*
  at Wilton 1920s
  24 × 29 in.
  Unsigned
  The Studio, Chartwell

119 *Venice, the Bridge of Sighs c. 1920*
  21 × 14 in. Canvas board
  Unsigned
  The Studio, Chartwell

120 *The Palladian bridge at Wilton 1920s*
$23\frac{3}{4} \times 17\frac{1}{2}$ in.
Initialled
COLLECTIONS: Captain Oswald Frewen
Mrs Oswald Frewen
Sold Parke-Bernet 9th December 1965

XX (121) *The Palladian bridge at Wilton*
c. 1925
25×30 in.
Initialled
COLLECTION:
Lady Spencer–Churchill
Earl of Pembroke

XXI (122) *Palladian bridge c. 1925*
Reproduced by gracious permission of Her Majesty the Queen
25×30 in.
Initialled
EXHIBITIONS: World Tour 1958
Royal Academy 1959
COLLECTION:
The Queen's Private Collection

125

123 *The water garden at Chartwell c. 1925*
    20 × 14 in. Canvas board
    Initialled
    The Studio, Chartwell

124 *Marrakech c. 1935*
    24 × 20 in.
    Initialled
    COLLECTION: Hudson's Bay Company

125 *Terrace at Hever c. 1922*
    13¾ × 18¼ in. Canvas board.
    Unsigned
    The Studio, Chartwell

126 *The swimming pool at Mme Balsan's*
house in Florida 1930s
25 × 30 in.
Unsigned
The Studio, Chartwell

127 *Marrakech c. 1935*
20 × 14 in. Canvas board
Unsigned
The Studio, Chartwell

128 *Marrakech c. 1935*
19¾ × 14 in. Canvas board
Unsigned
The Studio, Chartwell

129 *Seascape c. 1925*
    13 × 16 in. Panel
    Unsigned
    Unfinished copy of a
    picture (133) hanging in
    Sir Winston's study at Chartwell
    The Studio, Chartwell

130 *San Giorgio, Venice 1920s*
    20 × 24 in.
    Unsigned
    The Studio, Chartwell

131 *Harbour in the south of France c. 1925*
    14 × 20 in. Canvas board
    Unsigned
    The Studio, Chartwell

132 *The coast near Antibes c. 1925*
    25 × 30 in.
    Unsigned
    COLLECTIONS: Mr R. E. Golding
    Mr Harry Kay
    Sold Christie's 4th November, 1966
    Mr R. A. Sampson

133 *Seascape 1920s*
  20 × 24 in.
  Unsigned
  The Studio, Chartwell

XXII (134) *Flat calm with a high-prowed*
  boat c. 1925
  23½ × 32 in.
  Unsigned
  The Studio, Chartwell

XXIII (135) *The Adriatic with Venice in*
  the distance c. 1925
  25 × 30 in.
  Initialled
  The Studio, Chartwell
  COLLECTION:
  Harrow School

XXIV (136) *The Firth of Forth c. 1925*
  25 × 30 in.
  Unsigned
  The Studio, Chartwell

137 *The loggia, Esher Place, Surrey 1920s*
  20 × 24 in.
  Initialled
  EXHIBITION:
  New York World's Fair 1965
  COLLECTION:
  Lord Hailes

138 *Near Salzburg 1920s*
  20 × 24 in.
  Initialled
  The Studio, Chartwell

139 *Near Salzburg c. 1920*
  14 × 20 in. Canvas board
  Unsigned
  The Studio, Chartwell

XXV (140) *Le Moulin,*
  St-Georges-Motel c. 1923
  24 × 18 in.
  Initialled
  COLLECTION:
  Lady Spencer-Churchill
  Mrs G. M. Kennedy

142

143

XXVI (141) *The entrance to a drive*
     c. 1920
     27 × 22 in.
     Initialled
     The Studio, Chartwell

142 *Winter sunshine, Chartwell c. 1924*
     14 × 20 in. Millboard. Signed
     ILLUSTRATED:
     Painting as a Pastime
     EXHIBITIONS:
     Royal Academy 1947
     World Tour 1958
     Royal Academy 1959
     COLLECTION:
     Lady Spencer-Churchill

143 *At Lullenden Manor*
     c. 1922
     20 × 24 in.
     Initialled
     The Studio, Chartwell

XXVII (144) *Pergola at Chartwell c. 1925*
     24 × 20 in.
     Initialled
     The Studio, Chartwell

XXVIII (145) *Chequers on an autumn evening c. 1928*
20 × 24 in.
Unsigned
The Studio, Chartwell

146 *The garden at Hoe Farm with Lady Gwendeline Churchill c. 1915*
20 × 24 in.
Unsigned
The Studio, Chartwell
COLLECTION:
Mrs Christopher Soames

147 *Trees and shadows c. 1928*
20 × 14 in. Canvas board
Initialled
The Studio, Chartwell

148 *Landscape with a small pool 1920s*
20 × 24 in.
Initialled
COLLECTION: Mr Charles Clore
(From a previous owner)

149 *Hoe Farm 1915*
20 × 24 in.
Unsigned
The Studio, Chartwell

XXIX (150) *Snow at Chartwell 1924*
24 × 32 in.
Unsigned
EXHIBITIONS: World Tour 1958
Royal Academy 1959
New York World's Fair 1965
COLLECTION: Mr Randolph Churchill

XXX (151) *Lullenden Manor c. 1922*
30 × 25 in.
Unsigned
The Studio, Chartwell

152 *Lady Castlerosse c. 1930*
24 × 20 in.
Unsigned
The Studio, Chartwell

XXXI (153) *Green trees and poppies at Lullenden c. 1920*
29 × 24 in.
Initialled
The Studio, Chartwell

XXXII (154) *Magnolia c. 1930*
20 × 16 in.
Initialled
EXHIBITION:
New York World's Fair 1965
COLLECTION:
Sarah, Lady Audley

155 *Painting lesson from Mr Sickert c. 1930*
20 × 14 in.
Unsigned
Inscribed with the title on the back
The Studio, Chartwell

156 *Snow under arch, or, The messenger c. 1935*
24 × 20 in.
Initialled
COLLECTION:
Lady Spencer-Churchill

157 *The dining-room at Chartwell with*
Miss Diana Churchill 1933
$21\frac{3}{4} \times 25\frac{3}{4}$ in.
Unsigned
The Studio, Chartwell

158 *Viscountess Castlerosse relaxing on a terrace 1930s*
14×20 in.
Initialled (?)
COLLECTION: Marquess of Bath
(From the executor of a previous owner)

159 *The line out c. 1937*
20×16 in.
Unsigned
The Waratahs jumping for the ball
against the South of France at Toulouse.
The Studio, Chartwell

160 *The circus 1930s*
26 × 30 in.
Initialled
EXHIBITION : New York World's Fair 1965
COLLECTION : Hon. Lewis Douglas

161 *Performing elephants in the circus ring c. 1935*
25 × 30 in.
Unsigned
Bertram Mills Circus, Olympia, London 1928
The Studio, Chartwell
COLLECTION : Mr Rupert Soames

162 *After Daubigny 1930s*
20 × 30 in.
Unsigned
EXHIBITION : New York World's Fair 1965
COLLECTION : Mr Charles Clore
(From a previous owner)

163 *Copy of the picture by John Lewis Brown
hanging in the study at Chartwell c. 1930*
30 × 25 in.
Initialled
The Studio, Chartwell

164

165

166

164 *After Daubigny 1930s*
20 × 30 in.
'After Daubigny by W.S.C.'
COLLECTION: Earl of Birkenhead

165 *After Daubigny 1930s*
14 × 22 in.
Unsigned
COLLECTION: Mr Giles Romilly

166 *Studio still life c. 1930*
14 × 20 in. Canvas board
Unsigned
EXHIBITION: Royal Academy 1959
COLLECTION: Lady Spencer-Churchill

167 *Fruit and reflections 1930s*
14½ × 22 in.
Initialled
COLLECTION : Earl de la Warr

XXXIII (168) *A loaf of bread c. 1930*
14 × 21 in.
Unsigned
COLLECTION : Mr Randolph Churchill

169 *Still life, fruit 1930s*
   25 × 30 in. estimated
   Initialled
   COLLECTIONS: Mrs Diana Sandys
   Mr Julian Sandys

170

171

172

173

170 *Flowers in a white bowl c. 1930*
20 × 24 in.
Unsigned
The Studio, Chartwell

171 *Flowers in a blue vase c. 1935*
20 × 24 in.
Unsigned
The Studio, Chartwell

172 *Nasturtiums in a silver
presentation bowl c. 1935*
18 × 24 in.
Unsigned
COLLECTION: Lady Spencer-Churchill

173 *Still life, silver 1930s*
14 × 19½ in.
Initialled
COLLECTION: Earl of Avon

174

175

176

177

174 *Silver life c. 1930*
   14 × 20 in. Canvas board
   Unsigned
   The Studio, Chartwell

175 *Silver life c. 1930*
   14 × 20 in. Canvas board
   Unsigned
   The Studio, Chartwell

176 *Jug and bottles 1930s*
   20 × 14 in.
   Initialled
   EXHIBITION: New York World's Fair 1965
   COLLECTION: Hon. and Mrs Averell Harriman

177 *Bottlescape c. 1932*
   28 × 36 in.
   Initialled
   EXHIBITIONS: World Tour 1958
   Royal Academy 1959
   COLLECTION: Lady Spencer–Churchill

178 *Mallows c. 1930*
24 × 20 in.
Initialled
ILLUSTRATED: *Painting as a Pastime*
EXHIBITIONS: World Tour 1958
Royal Academy 1959
COLLECTION: Lady Spencer-Churchill

179

180

181

182

179 *Two glasses on a verandah (after Sargent) c. 1930*
$17\frac{1}{2} \times 14\frac{1}{2}$ in.
Unsigned
COLLECTION: Lady Spencer-Churchill

180 *Daffodils and tulips c. 1930*
27×20 in.
Unsigned
The Studio, Chartwell

181 *Study of roses 1930s*
20×14 in.
Initialled
COLLECTION: Vivien, Lady Olivier

182 *Magnolia c. 1930*
    20 × 16 in.
    Initialled
    COLLECTION: Mr Randolph Churchill

183 *Magnolia c. 1930*
    27 × 20 in.
    Initialled
    EXHIBITIONS: World Tour 1958
    Royal Academy 1959
    COLLECTION: Mrs Christopher Soames

184

185

186

187

184 *A corner of the drawing-room at Chartwell c. 1938*
20 × 24 in.
Unsigned
The Studio, Chartwell

185 *Wilton, the long gallery c. 1930*
24 × 20 in.
Initialled
The Studio, Chartwell

186 *Interior at Breccles c. 1930*
25 × 23½ in.
Initialled
COLLECTION: Lady Spencer-Churchill

187 *Interior at Breccles c. 1935*
   24 × 20 in.
   Initialled
   The Studio, Chartwell

188 *The cloisters c. 1930*
   20 × 24 in.
   Unsigned
   The Studio, Chartwell

XXXIV (189) *The dining-room of Sir Philip Sassoon's*
   house at Lympne c. 1930
   24 × 20 in.
   Initialled
   The Studio, Chartwell

190

191

192

190 *Italian lake scene c. 1935*
   22 × 28 in.
   Unsigned
   The Studio, Chartwell

191 *In the Dolomites c. 1935*
   14 × 20 in. Canvas board
   Initialled
   The Studio, Chartwell

192 *Loch scene on the Duke of
   Sutherland's estate c. 1930*
   22 × 28 in.
   Unsigned
   The Studio, Chartwell

193 *View at Lochmore c. 1935*
20 × 24 in.
Unsigned
The Studio, Chartwell
COLLECTION:
Anne, Duchess of Westminster

194 *A loch on the Duke of Sutherland's estate c. 1935*
20 × 24 in.
Unsigned
The Studio, Chartwell
COLLECTION: Mr Anthony Montague Browne

195 *Mountain near Lochmore c. 1935*
30 × 25 in.
Initialled
The Studio, Chartwell

196 *The Valley of the Ourika c. 1935*
  26 × 32 in.
  Unsigned
  COLLECTION: Lady Spencer-Churchill

197 *Scene in Morocco 1930s*
  13 × 19 in.
  Initialled
  COLLECTION: Hon. Mrs Henley

198 *View in the Italian Alps c. 1934*
  25 × 30 in.
  Initialled
  The Studio, Chartwell

199 *Coast scene on the Riviera c. 1930*
20 × 24 in.
Unsigned
The Studio, Chartwell

200

201

202

203

200 *View in the Italian Alps c. 1934*
    20 × 24 in.
    Initialled
    COLLECTION:
    Lady Spencer-Churchill

201 *Mountainous lake scene c. 1935*
    25 × 30 in.
    Unsigned
    The Studio, Chartwell

202 *La Montagne, St Victoire c. 1935*
    25 × 30 in.
    Initialled
    The Studio, Chartwell

203 *View of Eze, Alpes-Maritimes c. 1930*
    26 × 32 in.
    Unsigned
    The Studio, Chartwell

204 *View of Eze c. 1930*
30 × 25 in.
Unsigned
The Studio, Chartwell

205 *Loire château c. 1935*
20 × 24 in.
Initialled
The Studio, Chartwell

206 *Battlements at Carcassonne
1930s*
10 × 8 in. estimated
Unsigned
COLLECTION:
Mrs Christopher Soames

207 *View near Vence, Alpes-Maritimes c. 1935*
20 × 24 in.
Unsigned
The Studio, Chartwell

208 *Carcassonne, southern France c. 1930*
20 × 24 in.
Unsigned
The Studio, Chartwell

209 *Distant view of Eze c. 1930*
20 × 30 in.
Unsigned
The Studio, Chartwell

210

211

212

213

210 *Summer landscape in the south of France c.1930*
28 × 36 in.
Unsigned
COLLECTION: Lady Spencer-Churchill

211 *Sunset over the Atlas Mountains c.1935*
20 × 24 in.
Unsigned
The Studio, Chartwell

212 *Ramparts of Rhodes 1930s*
14 × 20 in.
Unsigned
COLLECTION:
Mr Winston Churchill

213 *Scene at Marrakech c.1935*
23¼ × 36 in.
Initialled
COLLECTION:
Field Marshal Viscount Montgomery

214 *Marrakech 1935–6*
25 × 30 in.
Initialled
COLLECTIONS: Lord Beaverbrook
Beaverbrook Art Gallery

XXXV (215) *View of Carcassonne,*
southern France c. 1930
25 × 30 in.
Initialled
The Studio, Chartwell

XXXVI (216) *The battlements at Rhodes 1930–38*
25 × 30 in.
Unsigned
COLLECTION: Mr Randolph Churchill

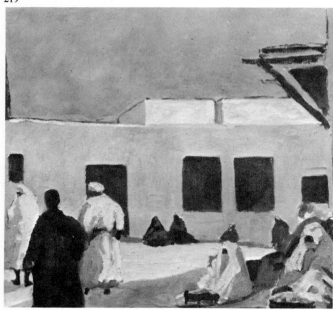

217 *Marrakech c. 1935*
   20 × 14 in. Canvas board
   Unsigned
   The Studio, Chartwell

218 *Marrakech c. 1935*
   18 × 24 in.
   Unsigned
   The Studio, Chartwell

219 *Marrakech c. 1935*
   16½ × 18 in.
   Unsigned
   The Studio, Chartwell

220 *Marrakech c. 1935*
   21½ × 26½ in.
   Initialled
   COLLECTION: Miss Elizabeth Navarro

221 *The garden entrance at Lympne c. 1930*
Unsigned
The Studio, Chartwell

XXXVII (222) *The terrace at Lympne c. 1930*
25 × 30 in.
Initialled
The Studio, Chartwell

223

224

225

223 *Porch at Cranborne c. 1935*
20 × 14 in. Canvas board
Initialled
The Studio, Chartwell

224 *The gate at Marrakech c. 1935*
19½ × 21¼ in.
Initialled
Sold anonymously Parke-Bernet
8th December 1965

225 *The house at Lympne c. 1932*
20 × 30 in.
Unsigned
The Studio, Chartwell

226 *North porch at the Manor House, Cranborne 1930s*
24 × 20 in.
Initialled
COLLECTION: Marquess of Salisbury

227 *An English garden in summer, with Lady Eleanor Smith c. 1930*
    24 × 20 in.
    Unsigned
    The Studio, Chartwell

228

229

230

228 *Shadows on the wall of a village in the south of France c. 1930*
24 × 20 in.
Unsigned
The Studio, Chartwell

229 *Farm at the head of Lake Como c. 1935*
20 × 24 in.
Unsigned
Inscribed on the back:
'Painted by my Husband.
Clementine S. Churchill'
The Studio, Chartwell

230 *Château St-Georges-Motel c. 1930*
18 × 22 in.
Unsigned
The Studio, Chartwell

231 *The mill at La Colle, with Sarah
and Randolph Churchill c. 1936–9*
$29\frac{3}{4} \times 24\frac{1}{2}$ in.
Initialled
COLLECTIONS: Miss Maxine Elliott
Lady Forbes-Robertson
Mrs E. Rivers-Bulkeley
Sold Sotheby's, 15th December 1965

XXXVIII (232) *Château St-Georges-Motel c. 1935*
20×24 in.
Initialled
COLLECTION: Mrs Christopher Soames

233

234

235

236

233 *The mill at St-Georges-Motel c. 1930*
20 × 24 in.
Unsigned
The Studio, Chartwell

234 *The mill at St-Georges-Motel c. 1930*
24 × 32 in. estimated
Initialled
ILLUSTRATED: *Painting as a Pastime*
COLLECTIONS: Mrs Diana Sandys
Mr Julian Sandys

235 *Ightham Mote 1930s*
$19\frac{1}{2}$ × $23\frac{1}{4}$ in.
Initialled
COLLECTIONS:
General Sir Ian Hamilton
Mr Ian Hamilton
Sold Sotheby's, 20th April 1966

236 *An open staircase in the south of France c. 1935*
16 × 20 in.
Unsigned
The Studio, Chartwell

237 *The ruins at Pompeii c. 1935*
  25 × 30 in.
  Unsigned
  The Studio, Chartwell

238 *St Jean de Vie 1930s*
  Pencil sketch on the back
  20 × 24 in.
  Initialled
  The Studio, Chartwell

239 *A ruined basilica c. 1930*
  20 × 14 in. Canvas board
  Unsigned
  The Studio, Chartwell

240 *A church, probably in the south of France c. 1935*
  22 × 18 in.
  Unsigned
  The Studio, Chartwell

241 *St Jean de Vie, between Cannes and Grasse 1930s*
20 × 24 in.
Initialled
The Studio, Chartwell

242 *A church in the south of France 1930s*
25½ × 20½ in.
Unsigned
COLLECTION : Miss Marryott Whyte

243 *Road in the south of France c. 1930*
18 × 11½ in. Board.
Unsigned
The Studio, Chartwell

244 *Nôtre Dame de Vie above Cannes 1930s*
20 × 24 in.
Initialled
EXHIBITION : New York World's Fair 1965
COLLECTIONS : Mrs Diana Sandys
Mrs Piers Dixon

246

245 *The porch of Nôtre Dame de Vie 1930s*
    30 × 20 in.
    Unsigned
    The Studio, Chartwell

246 *The gardener's cottage at Mme Balsan's*
    house in the south of France 1930s
    21 × 25 in.
    Unsigned
    COLLECTION : Miss Madeline Whyte

173

247 *Pont du Gard, Nîmes c. 1930*
    30 × 25 in.
    Initialled
    The Studio, Chartwell

248 *Calanques, near Marseilles 1930s*
    24 × 30 in.
    Unsigned
    COLLECTION: Lady Spencer-Churchill

249 *A village fête, St-Georges-Motel c. 1930*
    20 × 24 in.
    Initialled
    COLLECTION: Lady Spencer-Churchill

250 *On the Rhine c. 1930*
   14 × 20 in. Canvas board
   Unsigned
   The Studio, Chartwell

251 *Formal garden and pavilion at Lympne c. 1930*
   20 × 14 in. Canvas board
   Unsigned
   The Studio, Chartwell

252 *A field of tulips c. 1932*
   14 × 20 in. Canvas board
   Initialled
   The Studio, Chartwell

253 *Eastern garden scene c. 1930*
   27 × 23 in.
   Unsigned
   The Studio, Chartwell

254 *Colonnaded and paved walk at Hever c. 1930*
   24 × 20 in.
   Initialled
   The Studio, Chartwell

255 *At Eaton Hall, Chester 1930s*
   20 × 24 in.
   Unsigned
   COLLECTION: Mrs Christopher Soames

XXXIX (256) *In the Italian garden at Hever c. 1930*
   24 × 20 in.
   Initialled
   COLLECTION: Lady Spencer-Churchill

XL (257) *Summer house at Trent Park c. 1930*
   25 × 30 in.
   Initialled
   The Studio, Chartwell

258

259

260

261

258 *The colonnaded terrace at Hever c. 1930*
25 × 30 in.
Unsigned
The Studio, Chartwell

259 *View through an arch at Hever c. 1930*
24 × 20 in.
Unsigned
The Studio, Chartwell

260 *Trees in the eastern counties, near Breccles c. 1936*
25 × 30 in.
Unsigned
Inscribed on the back: 'Painted by my husband.
Clementine S. Churchill'
EXHIBITION: Royal Academy 1959
COLLECTIONS: Lady Spencer-Churchill
Mrs G. M. Kennedy

261 *English garden scene c. 1930*
  30 × 20 in.
  Unsigned
  The Studio, Chartwell

262 *Fountain in the garden at Hever c. 1938*
  20 × 26 in.
  Unsigned
  The Studio, Chartwell

263

264

265

263 *Terrace near Florence c. 1935*
　20 × 24 in.
　Unsigned
　Inscribed in pencil on the back:
　'Painted by my husband. Clementine S. Churchill'
　The Studio, Chartwell

264 *Riviera scene 1930s*
　17½ × 25½ in.
　Initialled and inscribed on the back
　EXHIBITION: New York World's Fair 1965
　COLLECTION: Mr G. Huntington Hartford
　Sold Sotheby's, 20th April 1966

265 *Garden on the Riviera c. 1935*
　25 × 30 in.
　Unsigned
　The Studio, Chartwell

266 *Lakeland landscape near Breccles 1930s*
24 × 20 in.
Initialled
COLLECTION: Lady Spencer-Churchill

267

267 *La Dragonnière, Cap Martin 1930s*
 24 × 29½ in.
 Signed
 COLLECTIONS: Lady Spencer-Churchill
 Sotheby's Charity Auction, 26th April 1961
 Mrs A. M. Oppenheim
 Sold Sotheby's, 20th April 1966

XLI (268) *Olive trees, Cap Martin c. 1934*
 25 × 30 in.
 Initialled
 EXHIBITIONS: World Tour 1958
 Royal Academy 1959
 COLLECTION: Mrs Christopher Soames

269 *Blenheim Palace through the branches
 of a cedar c. 1930*
 24 × 20 in.
 Initialled
 The Studio, Chartwell

269

270

271

272

270 *Villa on Cap Martin c. 1934*
   24 × 20 in.
   Initialled
   COLLECTIONS: Lady Spencer-Churchill
   Mrs Hill

271 *The sunken garden of La Dragonnière,*
   Cap Martin 1930s
   20 × 30 in.
   Initialled
   The Studio, Chartwell

272 *Olive grove, La Dragonnière c. 1934*
   $21\frac{3}{4} \times 27\frac{1}{2}$ in.
   Initialled
   ILLUSTRATED: *Painting as a Pastime*
   COLLECTION: Mr Winston Churchill

183

273

274

275

273 *A North African town c. 1930*
    25 × 30 in.
    Initialled
    The Studio, Chartwell

274 *Avenue, Trent Park c. 1930*
    20 × 24 in.
    Initialled
    EXHIBITIONS: World Tour 1958
    Royal Academy 1959
    COLLECTIONS: Lady Spencer-Churchill
    Mr Nicholas Soames

275 *The pergola at Trent Park c. 1930*
    25 × 30 in.
    Unsigned
    The Studio, Chartwell

276 *An avenue at Frinton-on-Sea,*
Essex, with Miss Diana Churchill c. 1922
20 × 24 in.
Initialled
The Studio, Chartwell

XLII (277) *Terrace at Trent Park c. 1935*
24 × 20 in.
Initialled
The Studio, Chartwell

278 *Pergola overlooking a lake c.1930*
    24 × 29 in.
    Unsigned
    The Studio, Chartwell

280

281

279 *View of Monte Carlo and Monaco c. 1930*
25 × 30 in.
Initialled
The Studio, Chartwell

280 *View of Monte Carlo c. 1935*
20 × 24 in.
Unsigned
The Studio, Chartwell

281 *Monte Carlo and Monaco c. 1930*
20 × 30 in.
Unsigned
The Studio, Chartwell

282 *View from the stone terrace at Lympne c. 1932*
    25 × 30 in.
    Unsigned
    The Studio, Chartwell

283 *Valley in the south of France c. 1935*
    25 × 30 in.
    Unsigned
    The Studio, Chartwell

284 *The Weald of Kent under snow.*
    Painted from Chartwell c. 1935
    20 × 24 in.
    Unsigned
    Inscribed: 'Given to Mary Churchill 1937'
    ILLUSTRATED: *Painting as a Pastime*
    COLLECTION: Mrs Christopher Soames

285 *An English valley c. 1935*
    20 × 24 in.
    Unsigned
    The Studio, Chartwell

XLIII (286) *View of Chartwell c. 1938*
    24 × 36 in.
    Unsigned
    Inscribed on the back:
    'Painted by my husband.
    Clementine S. Churchill'
    The Studio, Chartwell

XLIV (287) *Chartwell in winter, mid-1930s*
    25 × 30 in.
    Unsigned
    COLLECTION : Mrs Christopher Soames

288 *Landscape near Lympne c. 1930*
24 × 20 in.
Unsigned
The Studio, Chartwell

289 *Coast scene near Lympne c. 1930*
24 × 20 in.
Unsigned
The Studio, Chartwell

290 *Coast scene near Lympne c. 1930*
20 × 24 in.
Unsigned
The Studio, Chartwell

291 *Coast scene on the Riviera c. 1935*
20 × 24 in.
Initialled
The Studio, Chartwell

292 *Coast scene near Lympne in summer c. 1930*
20 × 24 in.
Initialled
The Studio, Chartwell

293 *South-west view of the sea from a
cliff top at Lympne c. 1935*
24 × 20 in.
Unsigned
The Studio, Chartwell

294 *Fishing port of Madeira 1930s*
22½ × 27½ in.
Unsigned
COLLECTION:
Mr Randolph Churchill

295 *Riviera coast scene c. 1935*
25 × 30 in.
Unsigned
The Studio, Chartwell

296 *Amsterdam harbour from
Lord Beaverbrook's yacht c. 1938*
13½ × 19 in.
Initialled
COLLECTION: Mr Walter Graebner
Sold Christie's, 13th May 1966

297 *Near Venice 1930s*
25 × 30 in.
Initialled
COLLECTION:
The late Mr Arthur Hays Sulzberger

298 *Study of boats c. 1933*
20 × 24 in.
Initialled
EXHIBITIONS: World Tour 1958
Royal Academy 1959
New York World's Fair 1965
COLLECTION: Lady Spencer-Churchill

299 *Harbour scene c. 1935*
20 × 24 in.
Initialled
The Studio, Chartwell
COLLECTION: Sir Leslie Rowan

300 *Boats in Cannes Harbour 1930s*
24 × 30 in.
Initialled
EXHIBITION: New York World's Fair 1965
COLLECTIONS: Mrs Diana Sandys
Mrs Piers Dixon

301 *Near Antibes c. 1930*
20 × 24 in.
Initialled
ILLUSTRATED: *Painting as a Pastime*
COLLECTION: Sir Robert Menzies

302 *Canal scene c. 1938*
    20 × 24 in.
    Signed
    EXHIBITION: New York World's Fair 1965
    COLLECTIONS: Mrs Victor Oliver
    Sold Parke-Bernet, 14th April 1965
    Mr Joyce C. Hall

303 *Harbour in the south of France c. 1930*
    18 × 26 in.
    Unsigned
    The Studio, Chartwell

304 *Boats in Cannes Harbour c. 1933*
    21 × 25 in.
    Signed
    EXHIBITIONS: World Tour 1958
    Royal Academy 1959
    COLLECTION: Lord Shawcross

305 *Sunset, Cannes c. 1933*
20 × 30 ins.
Initialled
EXHIBITIONS: World Tour 1958
Royal Academy 1959
COLLECTION: Lady Spencer-Churchill

306 *Harbour scene, Cannes 1930s*
26 × 30 in.
Unsigned
EXHIBITION: New York World's Fair 1965
COLLECTION: Sarah, Lady Audley

XLV (307) *Harbour scene in the south of France c. 1935*
20 × 24 in.
Unsigned
The Studio, Chartwell

308

308 *Boat in Cannes Harbour 1930s*
  20 × 30 in. estimated
  Unsigned (?)
  COLLECTIONS: Mrs Diana Sandys
  Mr Julian Sandys

XLVI (309) *Boats by a jetty on the Riviera 1930s*
  25 × 30 in.
  Unsigned
  The Studio, Chartwell

310 *Harbour, Cannes c. 1933*
  20 × 24 in.
  Initialled
  EXHIBITIONS: World Tour 1958
  Royal Academy 1959
  COLLECTION: Lady Spencer-Churchill

198

310

311

312

313

311 *Sunset in Cannes Harbour 1930s*
20 × 24½ in.
Unsigned
COLLECTION: Mr Randolph Churchill

312 *St-Jean-Cap-Ferrat 1930s*
18 × 26 in.
Initialled
EXHIBITION: New York World's Fair 1965
COLLECTION: Sarah, Lady Audley

313 *Château de l'Horizon, Cap Ferrat, early 1930s*
19½ × 29½ in.
Unsigned
COLLECTION: Dr S. Leonard Simpson
(From a previous owner)

314

315

316

317

314 *The club house and jetty at
St-Jean-Cap-Ferrat c. 1930*
26 × 32 in.
Unsigned
The Studio, Chartwell

315 *Late afternoon, St-Jean-Cap-Ferrat c. 1930*
26 × 32 in.
Initialled
The Studio, Chartwell

316 *The beach at Walmer c. 1938*
25 × 30 in.
Initialled
COLLECTION:
The late General Lord Ismay

317 *The Surf Club at Miami c. 1930*
24 × 32 in.
Unsigned
The Studio, Chartwell

318 *Beach scene on the Riviera 1930s*
20 × 24 in.
Unsigned
Inscribed in pencil on the back:
'Painted by my husband.
Clementine S. Churchill'
The Studio, Chartwell

319 *Coast scene, surf advancing on*
   to a sandy shore c. 1935
   25 × 30 in.
   Initialled
   The Studio, Chartwell

320 *The seashore 1930s*
   19¾ × 23¾ in.
   Unsigned
   COLLECTION:
   Mr W. Greenshields
   Sold Sotheby's, 20th April 1966

321 *The Atlantic near Biarritz*
   24 × 20 in.
   Initialled
   COLLECTIONS:
   Brendan Bracken
   Churchill College, Cambridge

322 *Distant view of Venice c. 1935*
   23 × 29 in.
   Unsigned
   The Studio, Chartwell

323 *Distant view of Venice c. 1935*
20 × 24 in.
Unsigned
The Studio, Chartwell

324 *Distant view of Venice c. 1935*
25 × 30 in.
Unsigned
The Studio, Chartwell

325 *Coast scene near Cannes c. 1935*
26 × 32 in.
Unsigned
The Studio, Chartwell

326 *Coast scene near Cannes c. 1930*
26 × 32 in.
Unsigned
The Studio, Chartwell

327 *Coast scene on the Riviera c. 1930*
26 × 32 in.
Unsigned
The Studio, Chartwell

328 *Castle on the Riviera c. 1935*
25 × 30 in.
Initialled
The Studio, Chartwell

329 *Coast scene on the Riviera c. 1930*
    25 × 30 in.
    Initialled
    The Studio, Chartwell

330 *Bay near Marseilles c. 1935*
    17¼ × 28¾ in.
    Initialled
    The Studio, Chartwell

331 *Coast scene near Marseilles c. 1935*
    13 × 16½ in. Panel
    Unsigned
    The Studio, Chartwell

332 *Mediterranean coast scene c. 1930*
20 × 27 in.
Initialled
COLLECTION: Lady Spencer-Churchill

333 *Near Marseilles c. 1930*
25 × 30 in.
Initialled
The Studio, Chartwell

XLVII (334) *Coast scene near Marseilles c. 1935*
25 × 30 in.
Initialled
The Studio, Chartwell

335

336

337

338

335 *Coast scene near Cap d' Ail c. 1935*
   25 × 30 in.
   Initialled
   The Studio, Chartwell

336 *Antibes 1930s*
   19¾ × 23¾ in.
   Unsigned
   COLLECTION: Mr W. Greenshields
   Sold Sotheby's, 20th April 1966

337 *Coast near Antibes c. 1933*
   26 × 32 in.
   Initialled
   The Studio, Chartwell

338 *Rocks near Cannes c. 1935*
   20 × 24 in.
   Unsigned
   The Studio, Chartwell

339 *Red rocks near Théoule, in the south of France c. 1933*
25 × 30 in.
Unsigned
The Studio, Chartwell

340

341

342

343

340 *Rocky scene in Sicily c. 1930*
    25 × 30 in.
    Initialled
    The Studio, Chartwell

341 *View through the arch of the*
    bridge over the Var c. 1930
    25 × 30 in.
    Unsigned
    The Studio, Chartwell

342 *Arch of bridge over the Var c. 1930*
    25 × 30 in.
    Initialled
    EXHIBITION: New York World's Fair 1965
    COLLECTIONS: Mrs Diana Sandys
    Mrs G. M. Kennedy

343 *Arch of the bridge over the Var,*
    sunset c. 1930
    25 × 30 in.
    Unsigned
    The Studio, Chartwell

344 *The goldfish pool at Chartwell 1932*
25 × 30 in.
Unsigned
ILLUSTRATED: *Painting as a Pastime*
EXHIBITIONS: World Tour 1958
Royal Academy 1959
COLLECTION: Lady Spencer-Churchill

XLVIII (345) *View from a bathing hut at Miami Surf Club c. 1932*
25 × 30 in.
Initialled
The Studio, Chartwell

346 *The lily pond at Coombe Place, Surrey c. 1930*
   20 × 14 in. Canvas board
   Initialled
   The Studio, Chartwell

347 *Sketch, probably on the Riviera c. 1930*
14 × 20 in. Canvas board
Initialled
The Studio, Chartwell

348 *The goldfish pool at Chartwell c. 1935*
Unfinished
25 × 30 in.
Initialled
The Studio, Chartwell

349 *Ornamental lily pool at Coombe Place, Surrey c. 1935*
14 × 20 in.
Initialled
The Studio, Chartwell

350 *Les Zoraides, Cap Martin 1935*
25 × 30 in.
Initialled
COLLECTION:
Lady Spencer-Churchill

351 *Les Zoraides, Cap Martin 1935*
20 × 24 in.
Initialled
EXHIBITIONS: World Tour 1958
Royal Academy 1959
New York World's Fair 1965
COLLECTION: Lady Birley

352 *The Loup River, Alpes-Maritime 1930*
20⅛ × 24 in.
Unsigned
ILLUSTRATED: *Painting as a Pastime*
EXHIBITION: Royal Academy 1947
COLLECTION: The Tate Gallery

353 *The canal at St-Georges-Motel 1930s*
19½ × 14 in.
Initialled
COLLECTION: Earl of Avon

354 *Avenue and formal pool at*
St-Georges-Motel c. 1935
24 × 20 in.
Initialled
The Studio, Chartwell

355 *In the park of the Château at*
St-Georges ·Motel 1930s
14 × 10 in.
Signed by: Paul Maze; A. D. de Segonzac;
Winston; Simon Levy; Ivor; Balsan;
all of whom contributed to the painting.
COLLECTION: Mr H. J. Chamberlain
Sold Sotheby's, 20th April 1966

XLIX (356) *English river landscape c. 1935*
24 × 20 in.
Initialled
COLLECTION: Lady Spencer-Churchill

357 *On the Var c. 1935*
      30 × 25 in.
      Initialled
      The Studio, Chartwell

L (358) *The Thames from Taplow c. 1935*
        30 × 25 in.
        Initialled
        COLLECTION:
        Lady Spencer-Churchill

359 *Tree-lined stream in England c. 1935*
      20 × 20 in.
      Unsigned
      The Studio, Chartwell

360 *River scene on the Loup c. 1930*
25 × 30 in.
Unsigned
The Studio, Chartwell

361 *River scene on the Loup c. 1930*
30 × 25 in.
Unsigned
COLLECTION: Lady Spencer-Churchill

362 *The Thames at Taplow c. 1935*
30 × 25 in.
Initialled
The Studio, Chartwell

LI (363) *Scene on the River Loup c. 1930*
18 × 22 in.
Unsigned
The Studio, Chartwell

217

364 *A lake in Norfolk c. 1936*
   24 × 20 in.
   Initialled
   EXHIBITIONS: World Tour 1958
   Royal Academy 1959
   COLLECTION: Lady Spencer-Churchill

LII (365) *A lake in Norfolk c. 1936*
   $22\frac{1}{2}$ × 20 in.
   Initialled
   COLLECTION: Lady Spencer-Churchill

366

367

368

369

366 *The garden at Wilton c. 1935*
$21\frac{1}{2} \times 17\frac{1}{4}$ in.
Initialled
The Studio, Chartwell

367 *Lake scene in Norfolk c. 1935*
20×24 in.
Unsigned
The Studio, Chartwell

368 *A pool on the Loup River c. 1930*
25×30 in.
Initialled
The Studio, Chartwell

369 *Lake scene in Norfolk c. 1935*
20×24 in.
Initialled
The Studio, Chartwell

370 *View in southern France c. 1935*
    20 × 24 in.
    Initialled
    The Studio, Chartwell

LIII (371) *Storm scene, south of France,*
    or, The bridge c. 1935
    25 × 30 in.
    Initialled
    COLLECTION: Lady Spencer-Churchill

372 *Lake near Breccles in autumn c. 1930*
    21½ × 29 in.
    Unsigned
    The Studio, Chartwell

372

373

374

375

373 *Near Breccles* *c.1930*
26 × 32 in.
Unsigned
The Studio, Chartwell

374 *The swimming pool at Chartwell* *c.1930*
Unfinished
19½ × 26 in.
Unsigned
COLLECTION : Lady Spencer-Churchill

375 *The swimming pool at Chartwell* *c.1935*
25 × 30 in.
Unsigned
The Studio, Chartwell

376

377

378

379

376 *Amaryllis lily 1940s*
36 × 24 in.
Initialled
COLLECTION:
Mrs Christopher Soames

377 *Buddha and lilies 1948*
40 × 30 in.
Initialled
EXHIBITION:
New York World's Fair 1965
COLLECTION:
Lady Spencer-Churchill

378 *Orchids c. 1948*
25 × 30 in.
Initialled
ILLUSTRATED: *Painting as a Pastime*
EXHIBITIONS: World Tour 1958
Royal Academy 1959
COLLECTION: Churchill College, Cambridge

379 *Black swans at Chartwell 1948*
28 × 22 in.
Initialled
COLLECTION: Mme Moatti
Sold Palais Galliera 1966

380 *Miss Cecily Gemmell c. 1949*
    24 × 18 in.
    Initialled 'WSC OB!'
    COLLECTION : Miss Cecily Gemmell

LIV (381) *Tower of Katoubia Mosque 1943*
    20 × 24 in.
    Initialled
    COLLECTIONS : President Roosevelt
    Mr Norman Hickman

LV (382) *Buddha and lily 1948*
    40 × 30 in.
    Initialled
    COLLECTION : Lady Spencer-Churchill

383 *Lakeside scene, Lake Como 1945*
   24 × 20 in.
   Initialled
   ILLUSTRATED: *Painting as a Pastime*
   COLLECTION: Lady Spencer-Churchill

LVI (384) *Black swans at Chartwell 1948*
   22 × 27 in.
   Initialled
   EXHIBITIONS: World Tour 1958
   Royal Academy 1959
   COLLECTION: Mr Randolph Churchill

LVII (385) *Water, Vaucluse 1948*
   18 × 24 in.
   Initialled
   EXHIBITIONS: World Tour 1958
   Royal Academy 1959
   COLLECTIONS: Lady Spencer-Churchill
   Captain Soames

386 *Fontaine de Vaucluse 1948*
  18 × 24 in.
  Initialled
  COLLECTION:
  Lady Spencer-Churchill

387 *Fontaine de Vaucluse 1948*
  25 × 30 in.
  Unsigned
  COLLECTION:
  Lady Spencer-Churchill

388 *Fontaine de Vaucluse c. 1948*
  23½ × 30 in.
  Unsigned
  COLLECTION:
  Lady Spencer-Churchill

389 *Water, Vaucluse 1940s*
  20 × 17¼ in.
  Unsigned
  The Studio, Chartwell

390 *Water, Vaucluse 1948*
24 × 18 in.
Initialled
COLLECTION: Lady Spencer-Churchill

LVIII (391) *Sketch of Lake Carezza, or,*
The twenty-minute sketch 1949
25 × 30 in.
Initialled
EXHIBITIONS: World Tour 1958
Royal Academy 1959
COLLECTION: Lady Spencer-Churchill

392 *Bridge near Aix-en-Provence 1948*
25 × 30 in.
Initialled
The Studio, Chartwell

392

393

394

395

393 *The bridge at Aix-en-Provence September 1948*
22 × 28 in.
Initialled
COLLECTIONS: Mr Willi Sax
Mrs M. Sax-Schlatter

394 *Lake Como 1948*
22 × 27 in.
Initialled
Painted in about an hour
COLLECTION: Lady Spencer-Churchill

395 *Lake Como 1945*
40 × 50 in.
Unsigned
EXHIBITIONS: World Tour 1958
Royal Academy 1959
COLLECTION: Lady Spencer-Churchill

396 *Scene on the River Meuse, with the artist 1946–7*
  25 × 30 in.
  Initialled
  The Studio, Chartwell

LIX (397) *Lake Geneva 1946*
  25 × 30 in.
  Initialled
  The Studio, Chartwell

398

399

400

401

398 *Lake Geneva and Mont Blanc 1940s*
    28 × 36 in.
    Initialled
    EXHIBITION: New York World's Fair 1965
    COLLECTION: Lord Moran

399 *The island on Lake Geneva,*
    from Choisy, with Mont Blanc 1946
    40 × 50 in.
    Unsigned
    The Studio, Chartwell

400 *Scene on the Meuse 1946–7*
    28 × 36 in.
    Unsigned
    The Studio, Chartwell

401 *Scene on the Meuse 1946–7*
    28 × 36 in.
    Unsigned
    The Studio, Chartwell

402

402 *Lake Garda 1940s*
   25 × 30 in.
   Initialled
   COLLECTION: Viscount Camrose

403 *Beaches near Antibes c. 1945*
   16 × 20 in.
   Initialled
   COLLECTION: Miss Horatia Seymour
   Sold Christie's, 12th November 1965

403

404

405

406

404 *Beaches near Antibes c. 1949*
   16 × 20 in.
   Unsigned
   The Studio, Chartwell

405 *Menaggio, Lake Como 1945*
   19½ × 29 in.
   Initialled
   COLLECTION: Mr G. C. Mason
   Sold Sotheby's, 24th May 1965

406 *Monte Carlo from Cap d' Ail, August 1949*
   22 × 27 in.
   Initialled
   The Studio, Chartwell

407 *Coast scene near Marseilles c. 1947*
 20 × 24 in.
 Initialled
 The Studio, Chartwell

408 *Lake Carezza in the Dolomites 1949*
 28 × 36 in.
 Unsigned
 The Studio, Chartwell

409 *Lake Carezza in the Dolomites 1940s*
16 × 22 in.
Initialled
The Studio, Chartwell

410 *Lake Carezza in the Dolomites August 1949*
26 × 30 in.
Initialled
COLLECTION: Lord Normanbrook

411 *Lake Carezza, Dolomites August 1949*
22 × 27 in.
Unsigned
COLLECTION: Lady Spencer-Churchill

412

413

414

415

412 *Lake Carezza in the Dolomites 1940s*
    25 × 30 in.
    Unsigned
    The Studio, Chartwell
    COLLECTION: The late Mr Anthony F. Moir

413 *By Lake Lugano 1945*
    22 × 28 in.
    Initialled
    ILLUSTRATED:
    Painting as a Pastime
    The Studio, Chartwell

414 *Canal scene near Bruges c. 1946*
    22 × 27 in.
    Initialled
    The Studio, Chartwell

415 *St-Jean-Cap-Ferrat 1946*
    20 × 24 in.
    Initialled
    ILLUSTRATED:
    Painting as a Pastime
    COLLECTION:
    Lady Spencer-Churchill

416 *The church by Lake Como September 1945*(?)
24 × 20 in.
Unsigned
ILLUSTRATED: *Painting as a Pastime*
COLLECTION: Lady Spencer-Churchill

417 *Harbour scene, probably on the Riviera c. 1947*
    24 × 18 in.
    Unsigned
    COLLECTION: Lady Spencer-Churchill

LX (418) *Torcello 1949*
    20 × 24 in.
    Initialled
    EXHIBITIONS: World Tour 1958
    Royal Academy 1959
    New York World's Fair 1965
    COLLECTION: Lady Spencer-Churchill

419 *Village scene, Lake Lugano September 1945*
20 × 30 in.
Initialled
ILLUSTRATED: *Painting as a Pastime*
EXHIBITION: New York World's Fair 1965
COLLECTION: The late Mr Anthony F. Moir

420 *Village near Lugano, with the artist at his easel 1945*
14 × 20 in. Canvas board
Unsigned
The Studio, Chartwell

421 *St-Jean-Cap-Ferrat 1946*
24 × 18 in.
Initialled
EXHIBITIONS: World Tour 1958
Royal Academy 1959
COLLECTION: Mr Winston Churchill

422 *Scene from the Venetian Causeway,*
  Miami Beach, Florida 1946
  25 × 30 in.
  Initialled
  COLLECTION : Colonel and Mrs Frank W. Clarke

423 *Lake Garda, San Vigilio August 1949*
  25 × 30 in.
  Initialled
  The Studio, Chartwell

423

424

425

426

424 *Frankfort Beach, Jamaica 1940s*
26 × 30 in.
Initialled
EXHIBITION : New York World's Fair 1965
COLLECTION : Mr Joyce C. Hall

425 *The Mediterranean near Genoa 1945*
18 × 22 in.
Initialled
ILLUSTRATED : *Painting as a Pastime*
EXHIBITIONS : World Tour 1958
Royal Academy 1959
COLLECTION : Lady Spencer-Churchill

426 *Rocky seascape 1940s*
22 × 27 in.
Initialled
COLLECTIONS : Earl Woolton
Lady Woolton

427

428

429

430

427 *Rocks near Cannes 1948*
  25 × 30 in.
  Initialled
  EXHIBITIONS: World Tour 1958
  Royal Academy 1959
  COLLECTIONS: Lady Spencer-Churchill
  Bristol University

428 *Marrakech c. 1949*
  25 × 30 in.
  Initialled
  The Studio, Chartwell

429 *Marrakech 1947*
  22 × 27 in.
  Initialled
  COLLECTIONS:
  Lady Spencer-Churchill
  Mr Julian Sandys

430 *Marrakech c. 1947*
  22 × 27 in.
  Initialled
  EXHIBITIONS: World Tour 1958
  Royal Academy 1959
  COLLECTION: Mr Winston Churchill

431 *Valley of the Ourika and Atlas Mountains 1948*
26 × 30 in.
Initialled
EXHIBITIONS: World Tour 1958
Royal Academy 1959
New York World's Fair 1965
COLLECTION: President Dwight D. Eisenhower

LXI (432) *Marrakech 1948*
25 × 30 in.
Initialled
COLLECTION:
Lady Spencer-Churchill

LXII (433) *Valley of the Ourika
near Marrakech 1948*
25 × 30 in.
Initialled
COLLECTION:
Lady Spencer-Churchill

434 *Marrakech 1940s*
    20 × 24 in.
    Initialled
    EXHIBITION : New York World's Fair 1965
    COLLECTION : President Harry S. Truman

436

437

435 *Mosque at Marrakech 1948*
   28 × 36 in.
   Unsigned
   Inscribed on the back:
   'Painted by my husband.
   Clementine S. Churchill'
   The Studio, Chartwell

436 *Near Marrakech 1940s*
   25 × 30 in.
   Initialled
   COLLECTION: Mr James Wood

437 *Village near Marrakech 1946*
   14 × 22 in.
   Unsigned
   The Studio, Chartwell

438 *Mosque at Marrakech 1948*
36 × 28 in.
Unsigned
COLLECTION: Lady Spencer-Churchill

439 *Scuola di S. Marco, Venice 1940s*
19½ × 24 in.
Initialled
COLLECTION: Mr Charles Graham-Dixon

440 *The ruins of Amiens Cathedral*
(after a Sargent) c. 1947
25 × 30 in.
Unsigned
The Studio, Chartwell

441 *On Cap Martin 1940s*
14 × 18 in.
Unsigned
The Studio, Chartwell

442 *Chartwell landscape with sheep 1940s*
28 × 21½ in.
Initialled
COLLECTION : The late Mr Henry R. Luce
Mrs Clare Boothe Luce

LXIII (443) *Le Béguinage, Bruges 1946*
25 × 30 in.
Initialled
EXHIBITIONS : World Tour 1958
Royal Academy 1959
COLLECTION : Miss Grace Hamblin

444 *Inland view from Choisy, Switzerland 1946*
22 × 20½ in.
Unsigned
The Studio, Chartwell

LXIV (445) *View from Chartwell c. 1948*
30 × 25 in.
Initialled
COLLECTIONS:
Lady Spencer-Churchill
Mr Winston Churchill

LXV (446) *Chartwell kitchen garden 1948*
25 × 30 in.
Unsigned
EXHIBITIONS: World Tour 1958
Royal Academy 1959
COLLECTION: Mrs Christopher Soames

447 *Broad landscape near Choisy 1940s*
Unfinished
46 × 77 in.
Unsigned
The Studio, Chartwell

448 *Distant view of a town in the south of France c. 1948*
22 × 27 in.
Initialled
The Studio, Chartwell

449 *Landscape in Provence (between Aix and Arles) c. 1947*
22 × 27 in.
Initialled (twice)
COLLECTION : Mr Edward Heath

450

451

452

453

450 *Vase of red tulips (after Cézanne)*
1957, at La Pausa
28½ × 16½ in.
Initialled
COLLECTION:
Mr and Mrs Emery Reves

451 *The Colleoni Memorial, Venice c. 1951*
21 × 19½ in.
Unsigned
COLLECTION:
Lady Spencer-Churchill

452 *Walls at Marrakech c. 1955*
30 × 25 in.
Unsigned
The Studio, Chartwell

453 *Marrakech, with a camel c. 1954*
22 × 27 in.
Unsigned
The Studio, Chartwell

454 *The Bargello in Florence c.1951*
24 × 20 in.
Initialled
COLLECTION: Lady Spencer-Churchill

LXVI (455) *Oranges and lemons 1958*
20 × 24 in.
Unsigned
Painted at La Pausa
EXHIBITIONS: Royal Academy 1958
New York World's Fair 1965
COLLECTIONS: Mrs Diana Sandys
Mrs G. M. Kennedy

LXVII (456) *Lady Churchill at the launching of
HMS Indomitable c.1954*
30 × 25 in.
Unsigned
Inscribed on the back:
'Painted by my husband.
Clementine S. Churchill'
The Studio, Chartwell
COLLECTION: Mr Winston Churchill

458

459

457 *Marrakech, a man leading a camel c. 1958*
    25 × 30 in.
    Initialled
    The Studio, Chartwell

458 *The Todhra Gorge, Morocco 1951*
    24 × 18 in.
    Initialled
    The Studio, Chartwell

459 *The Gorge at Todhra 1951*
    24 × 18 in.
    Initialled
    COLLECTION : Lady Spencer-Churchill

460 *Gate at Marrakech c. 1950*
20 × 16 in.
Unsigned
The Studio, Chartwell

LXVIII (461) *The Doge's Palace in Venice c. 1951*
24 × 20 in.
Initialled
COLLECTION : Lady Spencer-Churchill
Miss Arabella Churchill

LXIX (462) *Gate at Marrakech, a man
on a donkey c. 1950*
25 × 30 in.
Unsigned
The Studio, Chartwell

463 *Marrakech, a group of palms 1950s*
   28 × 21 in.
   Initialled
   COLLECTION: Mr and Mrs Henry Luce III

464 *Near Marrakech c. 1954*
   27 × 22 in.
   Initialled
   The Studio, Chartwell

465 *Garden at Marrakech c. 1955*
   25 × 30 in.
   Initialled
   The Studio, Chartwell

466 *Marrakech,*
   and the Atlas Mountains c. 1955
   25 × 30 in.
   Unsigned
   The Studio, Chartwell

467 *The garden of the Mamounia Hotel,*
Marrakech c. 1954
22 × 27 in.
Initialled
The Studio, Chartwell

468 *Marrakech c. 1955*
  18 × 30 in.
  Unsigned
  Inscribed on the back:
  'Painted by my husband.
  Clementine S. Churchill'
  The Studio, Chartwell

469 *The Plain of Timerhir 1951*
  22 × 27 in.
  Unsigned
  COLLECTIONS:
  Lady Spencer-Churchill
  4th (Queen's Own) Hussars

470 *The Valley of the Ourika c. 1954*
  22 × 27 in.
  Initialled
  The Studio, Chartwell

471 *Blue grass – La Capponcina 1954*
  25 × 30 in.
  Initialled
  The Studio, Chartwell
  COLLECTION: Dr Roberts

472 *La Capponcina 1950*
  25 × 30 in.
  Initialled
  COLLECTIONS: The late Lord Beaverbrook
  Beaverbrook Art Gallery

LXX (473) *Cap d'Ail 1952*
  30 × 25 in.
  Initialled
  COLLECTION: Lady Spencer-Churchill

474 *Villa on the Nivello c. 1952*
   20 × 24 in.
   Initialled
   COLLECTION: Lady Spencer-Churchill

LXXI (475) *The walled garden at La Capponcina c. 1955*
   25 × 30 in.
   Initialled
   The Studio, Chartwell

476 *Venice 1951*
  25 × 36 in. Millboard
  Initialled
  EXHIBITIONS: World Tour 1958
  Royal Academy 1959
  COLLECTIONS: Lady Spencer-Churchill
House of Commons

477 *La Maison Rouge, near Aix-en-Provence*
  (after Cézanne) 1955
  20 × 24 in.
  Unsigned
  The Studio, Chartwell

478 *Venice, canal scene c. 1951*
  Unfinished
  25 × 30 in.
  Unsigned
  The Studio, Chartwell

479 *River landscape near Venice c. 1950*
22 × 27 in.
Unsigned
Inscribed on the back:
'Painted by my husband near Venice.
Clementine S. Churchill'
The Studio, Chartwell

480

481

482

480 *Scene near Venice 1950s*
   25 × 30 in.
   Initialled
   The Studio, Chartwell

481 *Monte Carlo from Cap d'Ail c. 1955*
   25 × 30 in.
   Unsigned
   The Studio, Chartwell

482 *The lakes at Chartwell c. 1950*
   20 × 24 in.
   Unsigned
   COLLECTION: Lady Spencer-Churchill

483 *Leaning palm, Jamaica c. 1955*
  24 × 20 in.
  Initialled
  COLLECTION : Lady Spencer-Churchill

484

485

486

484 *Jamaican beach c. 1952*
20 × 19¼ in.
Unsigned
The Studio, Chartwell

485 *Red rocks 1951*
20 × 24 in.
Unsigned
EXHIBITION : New York World's Fair 1965
COLLECTIONS : Mrs Diana Sandys
Mrs G. M. Kennedy

486 *Red rocks in the south of France c. 1950*
20 × 24 in.
Initialled
The Studio, Chartwell

487

488

489

487 *The Grotto of Ropemakers, Syracuse 1955*
   25 × 30 in.
   Initialled
   The Studio, Chartwell

488 *Sea from La Capponcina 1954*
   24¾ × 30 in.
   Initialled
   EXHIBITIONS: World Tour 1958
   Royal Academy 1959
   COLLECTION: Mr Winston Churchill

489 *Cap d'Ail, Alpes–Maritimes 1950s*
   25 × 30 in.
   Initialled
   EXHIBITION:
   New York World's Fair 1965
   COLLECTION:
   Royal Academy of Arts. Diploma Work

490 *View on the Riviera c. 1950*
24 × 18 in.
Initialled
The Studio, Chartwell

491 *The custody of the child 1955*
　　24 × 30 in.
　　Initialled
　　EXHIBITIONS : World Tour 1958
　　Royal Academy 1959
　　COLLECTION : Mr and Mrs Emery Reves

492 *Sea and pine trees, Cap d' Ail 1950s*
　　26 × 30 in.
　　Unsigned
　　EXHIBITION : New York World's Fair 1965
　　COLLECTION : Mrs Blanche Russell

493 *Menton from La Pausa 1957*
　　26 × 29½ in.
　　Unsigned
　　COLLECTION : Lady Spencer-Churchill

LXXII (494) *View of Menton and Italy from La Pausa 1957*
24 × 30 in.
Initialled
EXHIBITION: New York World's Fair 1965
COLLECTION: Mr and Mrs Emery Reves

495 *Oscar Nemon 1954*
Height 13½ in.
Unique bronze cast
COLLECTION: Mr Oscar Nemon

496 *Oscar Nemon 1954*
Height 13½ in.
Unique plaster cast
The Studio, Chartwell

498

499

ADDENDA

497 *Scene in the south of France 1920s*
24½ × 29½ in.
Unsigned
COLLECTIONS: Lady Hawkey
Mrs Dinah M. Pratt

498 *View at Mimizan 1920s*
26 × 34 in.
Initialled
COLLECTION:
Anne, Duchess of Westminster

499 *Scene in the south of France,
possibly near Grasse 1930s*
25 × 30 in.
Initialled
COLLECTIONS: Viscount Horne
Miss Emily Horne
J. R. Lamberton

500 *Seascape near Antibes 1930s*
  20 × 24 in.
  Unsigned ?
  COLLECTION : Mr Antonio Giraudier

501 *Atlas Mountains from Marrakech c. 1949*
  30 × 25 in.
  Unsigned ?
  COLLECTION : Mr Antonio Giraudier

502 *Mimizan 1920s*
  30 × 25 in.
  Initialled
  COLLECTIONS : Mr Bernard Baruch
  Mr Harold Epstein
  Sold Parke-Bernet, 20th October 1966
  (*See overleaf*)

(*see* p. 267 for caption)

Paintings not illustrated

i *La Capponcina*
Details unknown
COLLECTIONS : Lord and Lady Beaverbrook
Lady Beaverbrook
Presented on the occasion of their
marriage, June 1963

ii, iii *Two views of the Giza Pyramids of Cairo* ;
one from a distance ; the other a close
up of Cheops and Khufu.
Both 27 × 35 in. Both initialled
Said to have been painted in November 1943
while returning from the
Teheran Conference. (?1920s)
COLLECTIONS : Field Marshal Smuts
The Smuts Family

iv *Landscape, perhaps at Chartwell*
$24\frac{1}{2} \times 29\frac{1}{2}$ in.
Initialled
COLLECTION : Mr Aristotle Onassis

INDEX

TITLES AND SUBJECTS

Numbers refer to the illustrations

OWNERS (*present or most recent*)

Anonymous purchasers through firms not indexed